John Updike
A Bibliography

John Updike

A Bibliography

By C. Clarke Taylor

Friends School of Baltimore

The Kent State University Press

The Serif Series:
Bibliographies and Checklists

William White, General Editor
Wayne State University

Copyright © 1968 by C. Clarke Taylor
All rights reserved
Library of Congress Card Catalogue Number 67-65584
Manufactured in the United States of America
at the press of The Oberlin Printing Company
Designed by Merald E. Wrolstad

First Edition

Introduction

Several twentieth century American writers have received outstanding critical acclaim in recent years. Few, however, have become more a subject of controversy than has John Updike. Each of his successive works has brought forth additional comment by all major critics as well as lengthy discussion in the popular press. His themes have been widely discussed in religious periodicals, and have been labeled both "shocking" and "subtle." He is accused of poor taste and of repellent characterization, yet his handling of language is considered unmatched by other American writers of his generation. Mr. Updike's rather unostentatious way of life and his continuous reflection upon a "typically American" youth has resulted in many biographical inquiries, as well as the suggestion that he reflects American society. It is of interest to note the developing British criticism of Mr. Updike. In addition, the Library of Congress has recently accepted the original manuscripts of *The Centaur* and *The Poorhouse Fair*, as well as certain notes and letters concerning Mr. Updike's work. In light of such attention it is astonishing to find no extensive listing of primary and secondary sources. David Galloway has prepared a checklist for his critical study, *The Absurd Hero in American Fiction* (B3), but this does not indicate purposeful representation of diverse criticism nor does it cover work by Mr. Updike previous to *New Yorker* publication. This listing and that prepared by Mr. Galloway should serve to complement each other.

This list covers work from 1949 thru July 1, 1967. An attempt has been made to accumulate a rather complete listing of primary sources. Every issue of the *Harvard Lampoon*, 1950-1954, Mr. Updike's years at Harvard, has been checked. In his early days as a student certain work contributed is unsigned and, although reasonably sure of that which belongs to Mr. Updike, I have chosen to include only credited work. In the case of the high school *Chatterbox*, only that work contributed by Mr. Updike during his senior year is included here due to his own desire to save only these issues. A more arbitrary means has been employed for inclusion of secondary material. An attempt has been made to cover the range of diversity which exists among critics concerning Mr. Updike's work. All periodical articles discovered have been included. In the case of reviews the tendency has been to include some of the less significant, especially from reputable periodicals, as well as the valuable. There exist a great many newspaper reviews and inclusion has been based solely upon my judgement of the source and/or the contents. Attempt has been made to cover criticism in various parts of the country, and to include newspapers from which reviews of several works have been found. Reviews from the Richmond, Va. *News Leader* and the Springfield *Republican* have not been annotated due to inaccessibility, but have been seen briefly by me at Alfred Knopf, publisher, and considered especially fine. Much has probably been overlooked: many articles covering a general topic of contemporary American literature, and possibly including Mr. Updike, have. not been exhaustively researched.

Two symbols are used throughout the bibliography: One asterisk (*) indicates failure to locate and investigate the source due either to time limitation or to inaccessibility to material. In most cases these are newspaper reviews, and have been seen only briefly in the Knopf files. Certain periodical entries, although investigated once and annotated, are still incomplete due to inability to re-locate them for the additional detail needed. Space has been left to indicate missing information. Likewise, certain reviews of *Verse* and *Carpentered Hen* have been forwarded to me by the respective publishers, and page numbers have not been affixed. Those entries marked with two asterisks (**) are borrowed from Mr. Galloway's checklist, and have not been seen by me either first hand or in any index.

Valuable material for this list has been located in the offices of Alfred A. Knopf and in the home of Mr. Updike's parents, Mr. and Mrs. Wesley Updike. Much credit is due these sources. I am also grateful to Dr. Jackson Bryer, at the University of Maryland, for continuous encouragement and advice. Most especially, appreciation is due John Updike for his willingness to supply necessary information, and for his patience in searching this tedious list for imperfections.

CLARKE TAYLOR

College Park, Maryland
September, 1967

A. Primary Sources
1. Books

A1 *The Carpentered Hen and Other Tame Creatures*. New York: Harper and Brothers, 1958.

A2 *The Poorhouse Fair*. New York: Alfred A. Knopf, 1959.

A3 *The Same Door*. New York: Alfred A. Knopf, 1959.
All of the stories in this collection first appeared in the *New Yorker*. They are entered below individually.

A4 *Rabbit, Run*. New York: Alfred A. Knopf, 1960.

A5 *The Magic Flute* by Wolfgang Amadeus Mozart. John Updike and Warren Chappell (adaptors and illustrators). New York: Alfred A. Knopf, 1962.

A6 *Pigeon Feathers*. New York: Alfred A. Knopf, 1962.
Contents: "Walter Briggs", "The Persistence of Desire", "Still Life", "Flight", "Should Wizard Hit Mommy?", "A Sense of Shelter", "Dear Alexandros", "Wife-Wooing", "Pigeon Feathers", "Home", "You'll Never Know, Dear, How Much I Love You", "The Astronomer", "A & P", "The Doctor's Wife", "Lifeguard", "The Blessed Man of Boston, My Grandfather's Thimble, And Fanning Island", "Packed Dirt, Churchgoing, A Dying Cat, A Traded Car"—all published in the *New Yorker*. "Archangel", "The Crow in the Woods"— first printed in *Big Table* and *The Transatlantic Review*, respectively.

A7 "John Updike (1940's)." In Martin Levin, ed. *Five Boyhoods*. New York: Doubleday, 1962, pp. 155-198. (Collected in *Assorted Prose* as "The Dogwood Tree")

A8 "Foreword." In *The Young King and Other Fairy Tales by Oscar Wilde.* New York: The Macmillan Co., 1962, pp. iii-v. (Collected in *Assorted Prose*)

A9 *The Centaur.* New York: Alfred A. Knopf, 1963.

A10 *Telephone Poles and Other Poems.* New York: Alfred A. Knopf, 1963.

A11 *The Ring* by Richard Wagner. John Updike and Warren Chappell (adaptors and illustrators). New York: Alfred A. Knopf, 1964.

A12 *Olinger Stories.* New York: Vintage, 1964.
All the stories in this collection first appeared in the *New Yorker.* They are entered individually below.

A13 *A Child's Calendar.* New York: Alfred A. Knopf, 1965.

A14 *Verse.* Greenwich, Conn.: Fawcett, 1965.
This collection includes all of the poems printed in *Telephone Poles* and *The Carpentered Hen.* One additional poem, "Forward," appears here for the first time.

A15 *Assorted Prose.* New York: Alfred A. Knopf, 1965.
This collection contains certain incidental, non-fictional prose that is not listed elsewhere in this Bibliography. Other material is entered individually below.

A16 *Of the Farm.* New York: Alfred A. Knopf, 1965.

A17 *Rabbit, Run* and *Poorhouse Fair.* New York: Modern Library, 1965.
The two novels, originally published individually (see A2 and A4), are reprinted in this volume.

A18 *The Music School.* New York: Alfred A. Knopf, 1966.
All the stories in this collection first appeared in the *New Yorker.* They are entered individually below.

2. Periodicals: Poetry

A19 "I Want a Lamp," *The American Courier*, X(July 1, 1949), 11.

A20 Untitled, Shillington, Pa. *Chatterbox*, September 15, 1949, p.8.

A21 "Inscription Upon Tombstone," Shillington, Pa. *Chatterbox*, September 23, 1949, p.8.

A22 "Out of Fashion," Shillington, Pa. *Chatterbox*, September 30, 1949, p.8.

A23 "To a Pair of Gone Glasses," Shillington, Pa. *Chatterbox*, October 28, 1949, p.8.

A24 "To Fred," Shillington, Pa. *Chatterbox*, November 4, 1949, p.8.

A25 "The Season of Mud," Shillington, Pa. *Chatterbox*, November 11, 1949, p.8.

A26 "Ballad Before the Newsreel," Shillington, Pa. *Chatterbox*, November 23, 1949, p.10.

A27 "Notes on Treatment of Typists," Shillington, Pa. *Chatterbox*, December 2, 1949, p.8.

A28 "A Sad, Sad Song," Shillington, Pa. *Chatterbox*, December 2, 1949, p.8.

A29 "Verses One Through Five," Shillington, Pa. *Chatterbox*, December 9, 1949, p.8.

A30 "A Christmas Carol for Cynics," Shillington, Pa. *Chatterbox*, December 22, 1949, p.10.

A31 "Greetings, Etc.," Shillington, Pa. *Chatterbox*, January 6, 1950, p.8.

A32 "Department of Amplification and Abomination," Shillington, Pa. *Chatterbox*, January 13, 1950, p.8.

A33 "From a Lemming," Shillington, Pa. *Chatterbox*, January 20, 1950, p.6.

A34 "The Moment Called Now," Shillington, Pa. *Chatterbox*, January 20, 1950, p.6.

A35 "Too Busy," Shillington, Pa. *Chatterbox*, January 27, 1950, p.8.

A36 "The Mags-I," Shillington, Pa. *Chatterbox*, January 27, 1950, p.8.

A37 "Transit Unions Reject Arbitration," Shillington, Pa. *Chatterbox*, February 3, 1950, p.8.

A38 "The Mags-II," Shillington, Pa. *Chatterbox*, February 3, 1950, p.8.

A39 "Obituary," Shillington, Pa. *Chatterbox*, February 10, 1950, p.8.

A40 "The Mags-III," Shillington, Pa. *Chatterbox*, February 10, 1950, p.8.

A41 "Valentine to the Hydrogen Bomb," Shillington, Pa. *Chatterbox*, February 10, 1950, p.8.

A42 "On the Last Day of the Season," Shillington, Pa. *Chatterbox*, February 17, 1950, p.8.

A43 "The Mags-IV," Shillington, Pa. *Chatterbox*, February 17, 1950, p.8.

A44 "Winter," Shillington, Pa. *Chatterbox*, February 24, 1950, p.8.

A45 "From a Lemming," Shillington, Pa. *Chatterbox*, February 24, 1950, p.8.

A46 "A Solid Geometry Student Looks at Learning," Shillington, Pa. *Chatterbox*, February 24, 1950, p.8.

A47 "The Mags-V," Shillington, Pa. *Chatterbox*, February 24, 1950, p.8.

A48 "The Boy Who Makes the Blackboard Squeak," *National Parent-Teacher* (February, 1950).

Although this work has never been located by me, notation of its publication is made in files kept by Mr. Updike.

A49 "Time is Circular in Shape," Shillington, Pa. *Chatterbox,* March 3, 1950, p.8.

A50 "The Mags-VI," Shillington, Pa. *Chatterbox,* March 3, 1950, p.8.

A51 "Logic," Shillington, Pa. *Chatterbox,* March 3, 1950, p.8.

A52 "Ode on a Pin Ball Machine," Shillington, Pa. *Chatterbox,* April 14, 1950, p.10.

A53 "The Mags-VIII," Shillington, Pa. *Chatterbox,* April 14, 1950, p.10.

A54 "Sonnet on Chaucer," Shillington, Pa. *Chatterbox,* April 14, 1950, p.10.

A55 "A-Headin' for the Break," Shillington, Pa. *Chatterbox,* April 21, 1950, p.2.

A56 "Wednesday Night Church Service," Shillington, Pa. *Chatterbox,* April 21, 1950, p.2.

A57 "While Awaiting Service in a Shoe Store," Shillington, Pa. *Chatterbox,* April 21, 1950, p.2.

A58 "The Mags-IX," Shillington, Pa. *Chatterbox,* April 21, 1950, p.6.

A59 "Yo-Yo Champ," Shillington, Pa. *Chatterbox,* April 28, 1950, p.8.

A60 "Child's Question," Shillington, Pa. *Chatterbox,* May 12, 1950, p.16.

A61 "Audience Participation: Everybody Sing," Shillington, Pa. *Chatterbox,* May 12, 1950, p.16.

A62 "Ha Ha Sam Spade You Slay Me," Shillington, Pa. *Chatterbox,* May 12, 1950, p.16.

A63 "Haunted House," Shillington, Pa. *Chatterbox*, May 12, 1950, p.16.

A64 "On F.M.," Shillington, Pa. *Chatterbox*, May 12, 1950, p.21.

A65 "Frank Advice to a Young Poet," Shillington, Pa. *Chatterbox*, May 12, 1950, p.22.

A66 "The Last Word," *Florida Magazine of Verse*, (Autumn, 1950).

A67 "Move Over Do Do," *Florida Magazine of Verse,* (Autumn, 1950).

A68 "The Lonely One," *Different*, (November-December, 1950).
  The three entries above, A66, A67, A68, have not been seen by me but notation of their publication has been located.

A69 "The Whale Shark," *Harvard Lampoon*, CXXXIX (November 24, 1950), 382.

A70 Untitled, *Harvard Lampoon*, CXL (February, 1951), 15.

A71 "Quick," Harvard Lampoon, CXL (May, 1951), 12.

A72 "The Men Who Live in Public Places," *Harvard Lampoon*, CXL (May, 1951), 18.

A73 "While Awaiting Service in a Shoe Store," *Harvard Lampoon*, CXL (May, 1951), 19. (See A57)

A74 "Timestyle," *Harvard Lampoon*, CXL (June, 1951), 11.

A75 "Call Him Mister," *Harvard Lampoon*, CXL (June, 1951), 17.

A76 "Modern Americans-I," *Harvard Lampoon*, CXL (September, 1951), 3.

A77 "Overheard in Widener," *Harvard Lampoon*, CXL (September, 1951), 12.

A78 "Fighting for Erie," *Harvard Lampoon*, CXL (October, 1951), 3.

A79 Untitled, *Harvard Lampoon*, CXL (October, 1951), 9.

A80 "Yo-Yo Champ," *Harvard Lampoon*, CXL (October, 1951), 6. (See A59)

A81 "Lingual Jingual," *Harvard Lampoon*, CXL (November, 1951), 3.

A82 "Skylard Story," *Harvard Lampoon*, CXL (November, 1951), 22.

A83 "Coiffure of Many Colors," *Harvard Lampoon*, CXL (December 22, 1951), 3.

A84 "Diamonds," *Harvard Lampoon*, CXL (December 22, 1951), 17.

A85 "Aged and Ailing," *Harvard Lampoon*, CXL (December 22, 1951), 20.

A86 "Modern Americans-II," *Harvard Lampoon*, CXLI (February, 1952), 12.

A87 "Letter to the Bravest of Them All," *Harvard Lampoon*, CXLI (March, 1952), 3.

A88 "Modern Americans-III," *Harvard Lampoon*, CXLI (March, 1952), 7.

A89 Untitled, *Harvard Lampoon*, CXLI (March, 1952), 9.

A90 "Lines Inscribed on a Piece of Caramel," *Harvard Lampoon*, CXLI (April, 1952), 9.

A91 Untitled, *Harvard Lampoon*, CXLI (April, 1952), 15.

A92 "Modern Americans-IV," *Harvard Lampoon*, CXLI (April, 1952), 22.

A93 "Outcast," *Harvard Lampoon*, CXLI (May, 1952), 2.

A94 "How to Watch a Crew Race," *Harvard Lampoon*, CXLI (May, 1952), 7.

A95 Untitled, *Harvard Lampoon*, CXLI (September, 1952), 7.

A96 "Lines in Favor of Deposed Kings," *Harvard Lampoon* CXLI (September, 1952), 15.

A97 "Il Penseroso," *Harvard Lampoon,* CXLI (October, 1952), 2.

A98 "Professor Harlow Shapley Warbles the Praises of Natural Sciences 115," *Harvard Lampoon,* CXLI (October, 1952), 19.

A99 "From a Young Democrat," *Harvard Lampoon,* CXLI (October, 1952), 19.

A100 Untitled, *Harvard Lampoon,* CXLI (December, 1952), 4.

A101 Untitled, *Harvard Lampoon,* CXLI (December, 1952), 7.

A102 Untitled, *Harvard Lampoon,* CXLII (February, 1953), 7.

A103 "The Population of Argentina," *Harvard Lampoon,* CXLII (February, 1953), 17. (Collected in *Carpentered Hen*)

A104 Untitled, *Harvard Lampoon,* CXLII (April, 1953), 7.

A105 "Mountain Impasse," *Harvard Lampoon,* CXLII (April, 1953), 11. (Collected in *Carpentered Hen*)

A106 "The Harvard Liberal Union Announces the Publication of the New Generation," *Harvard Lampoon,* CXLII (May, 1953), 19.

A107 "Lines," *Harvard Lampoon,* CXLII (May, 1953), 24.

A108 "First Edition," *Harvard Lampoon,* CXLII (June, 1953), 3.

A109 "Shrew Song," *Harvard Lampoon,* CXLII (June, 1953), 19.

A110 "Poetess," *Harvard Lampoon,* CXLII (September, 1953), 4. (Collected in *Carpentered Hen*)

A111 "The Summer Reader," *Harvard Lampoon*, CXLII (September, 1953), 7.

A112 "Lampy's Doggerel Guide to English Literature," *Harvard Lampoon*, CXLII (September, 1953), 12-13.

A113 "Tonsilorial Artist," *Harvard Lampoon*, CXLII (September, 1953), 15.

A114 "The Vowel and the Pusey-Cat," *Harvard Lampoon*, CXLII (September, 1953), 20.

A115 "The Hypocrite," *Harvard Lampoon*, CXLII (September, 1953), 23.

A116 "Lines on the Passing of the Jack-o-Lantern," *Harvard Lampoon*, CXLII (October, 1953), 9.

A117 "Married Men," *Harvard Lampoon*, CXLII (October, 1953), 11.

A118 "Footnotes to the Future," *Harvard Lampoon*, CXLII (October, 1953), 14. (Collected in *Carpentered Hen* under the title "Why the Telephone Wires Dip and the Poles are Cracked and Crooked")

A119 "This Isn't a Chain I'm Smoking," *Harvard Lampoon*, CXLII (October, 1953), 24.

A120 "Reverie," *Harvard Lampoon*, CXLII (December, 1953), 2-3.

A121 "I Like to Sing Also," *Harvard Lampoon*, CXLIII (February, 1954), 3.

A122 "Ballade for Subway Sitters," *Harvard Lampoon*, CXLIII (February, 1954), 23.

A123 "Coming Detractions," *Harvard Lampoon*, CXLIII (March, 1954), 18-19.

A124 Untitled, *Harvard Lampoon*, CXLIII (April, 1954), 9.

A125 "June 1954," *Harvard Lampoon*, CXLIII (June, 1954), 7.

A126 "Duet, with Muffled Brake Drums," *New Yorker*, XXX (August 14, 1954), 74. (Collected in *Carpentered Hen*)

A127 "Dilemma in the Delta," *Harvard Lampoon*, CXLIII (September, 1954), 22. (Collected in *Carpentered Hen*)

A128 "Love Song with Seven Piece Combo," *Harvard Lampoon*, CXLIII (December, 1954), 5.

A129 "Player Piano," *New Yorker*, XXX (December 4, 1954), 169. (Collected in *Carpentered Hen*)

A130 "Clan," *New Yorker*, XXX (December 18, 1954), 119. (Collected in *Carpentered Hen*)

A131 "Song of the Open Fireplace," *New Yorker*, XXX (January 8, 1955), 31. (Collected in *Carpentered Hen*)

A132 "Shipbored," *New Yorker*, XXX (January 15, 1955), 93. (Collected in *Carpentered Hen*)

A133 "Recitative for Punished Products," *Punch*, CCXXVII (February 9, 1955), 194. (Collected in *Carpentered Hen*)

A134 "March," *New Yorker*, XXX (February 12, 1955), 38. (Collected in *Carpentered Hen*)

A135 "Youth's Progress," *New Yorker*, XXXI (February 26, 1955), 28. (Collected in *Carpentered Hen*)

A136 "V. B. Nimble, V. B. Quick," *New Yorker,* XXXI (April 2, 1955), 36. (Collected in *Carpentered Hen*)

A137 "Lament, for Cocoa," *New Yorker*, XXXI (May 14, 1955), 163. (Collected in *Carpentered Hen*)

A138 "Humanities Course," *New Yorker*, XXXI (June 4, 1955), 100. (Collected in *Carpentered Hen*)

A139 "Sunglasses," *New Yorker*, XXXI (July 16, 1955), 65. (Collected in *Carpentered Hen*)

A140 "Imaginable Conference," *New Yorker*, XXXI (August 6, 1955), 24. (Collected in *Carpentered Hen*)

A141 "Sunflower," *New Yorker*, XXXI (September 10, 1955), 136. (Collected in *Carpentered Hen*)

A142 "Pooem," *New Yorker*, XXXI (October 1, 1955), 34. (Collected in *Carpentered Hen*)

A143 "Ode Fired Into Being by *Life*'s 48 Star Editorial," *New Yorker*, XXXI (October 15, 1955), 47. (Collected in *Carpentered Hen* under title "An Ode")

A144 "Superman," *New Yorker*, XXXI (November 12, 1955), 56. (Collected in *Carpentered Hen*)

A145 "To an Usherette," *New Yorker*, XXXI (December 10, 1955), 190. (Collected in *Carpentered Hen*)

A146 "Bitter Life," *New Yorker*, XXXI (January 7, 1956), 26. (Collected in *Carpentered Hen*)

A147 "Solid Comfort," *New Yorker*, XXXI (February 18, 1956), 93.

A148 "Tsokadze o altitudo," *New Yorker*, XXXII (February 25, 1956), 115. (Collected in *Carpentered Hen*)

A149 "Publius Vergilius Maro, the Madison Avenue Hick," *New Yorker*, XXXII (March 31, 1956), 32. (Collected in *Carpentered Hen*)

A150 "Mr. High-mind," *New Yorker*, XXXII (April 28, 1956), 44. (Collected in *Carpentered Hen*)

A151 "Little Poems," *New Yorker*, XXXII (July 21, 1956), 73. (Collected in *Carpentered Hen*)

A152 "Tao in the Yankee Stadium Bleachers," *New Yorker*, XXXII (August 18, 1956), 28. (Collected in *Carpentered Hen*)

A153 "Old Faces of '56," *New Yorker*, XXXII (October 27, 1956), 36. (Collected in *Carpentered Hen* under title "Popular Revivals, 1956")

A154 "Due Respect," *New Yorker*, XXXII (November 17, 1956), 50. (Collected in *Carpentered Hen*)

A155 "A Wooden Darning Egg," *Harper's*, CCXIII (December, 1956), 34. (Collected in *Carpentered Hen*)

A156 "Capacity," *New Yorker*, XXXII (January 5, 1957), 29. (Collected in *Carpentered Hen*)

A157 "Scansion from Exalted Heights," *New Yorker*, XXXII (February 9, 1957), 28-29.

A158 "Sensualist," *New Yorker*, XXXII (February 16, 1957), 30. (Collected in *Carpentered Hen*)

A159 "Scenic," *New Yorker*, XXXIII (March 9, 1957), 97. (Collected in *Carpentered Hen*)

A160 "A Rack of Paperbacks," *New Yorker*, XXXIII (March 23, 1957), 124. (Collected in *Carpentered Hen*)

A161 "Song in American Type," *New Yorker*, XXXIII (March 30, 1957), 30.

A162 "One-Year Old," *Ladies Home Journal*, LXXIV (March, 1957), 172. (Collected in *Carpentered Hen*)

A163 "Philological," *New Yorker*, XXXIII (April 6, 1957), 109. (Collected in *Carpentered Hen*)

A164 "Glasses," *New Yorker*, XXXIII (April 20, 1957), 139. (Collected in *Carpentered Hen*)

A165 "Modest Mound of Bones," *Commonweal*, LXVI (April 26, 1957), 92. (Collected in *Carpentered Hen*)

A166 "Planting a Mailbox," *New Yorker*, XXXIII (May 11, 1957), 103. (Collected in *Carpentered Hen*)

A167 "Ode III.ii: Horace," *Commonweal*, LXVI (June 7, 1957), 254. (Collected in *Carpentered Hen*)

A168 "Ex-Basketball Player," *New Yorker*, XXXIII (July 16, 1957), 62. (Collected in *Carpentered Hen*)

A169 "Even Egrets Err," *New Yorker*, XXXIII (September 7, 1957), 74. (Collected in *Carpentered Hen*)

A170 "Jack," *New Yorker*, XXXIII (October 19, 1957), 134.

A171 "Rm. 28, National Portrait Gallery, London," *New Yorker*, XXXIII (November 2, 1957), 40. (Collected in *Carpentered Hen* under title "Rm. 28")

A172 "Quilt," *New Yorker*, XXXIII (November 16, 1957), 54.

A173 "Reflection," *New Yorker*, XXXIII (November 30, 1957), 216.

A174 "Simple Life," *New Yorker*, XXXIII (January 18, 1958), 108.

A175 "Bendix," *New Yorker*, XXXIII (February 15, 1958), 30. (Collected in *Telephone Poles*)

A176 "Menagerie at Versailles in 1775," *Harper's*, CCXVI (May, 1958), 78. (Collected in *Telephone Poles*)

A177 "Reel," *New Yorker*, XXXIV (May 3, 1958), 133. (Collected in *Telephone Poles*)

A178 "Blked," *New Yorker*, XXXIV (June 21, 1958), 90.

A179 "Caligula's Dream," *Commonweal*, LXVIII (June 27, 1958), 327. (Collected in *Telephone Poles*)

A180 "Upon Learning That a Bird Exists Called the Turnstone," *New Yorker*, XXXIV (October 4, 1958), 39. (Collected in *Telephone Poles*)

A181 "Toothache Man," *New Yorker*, XXXIV (November 15, 1958), 58. (Collected in *Telephone Poles*)

A182 "Party Knee," *New Yorker*, XXXIV (December 13, 1958), 46. (Collected in *Telephone Poles*)

A183 "It Might Be Verse," *Reflections*, (1959), 10.
     This entry is incomplete because only the page on which this poem is printed has been seen in Mr. Updike's file, not the entire issue.

A184 "Moderate," *New Yorker*, XXXIV (January 10, 1959), 103. (Collected in *Telephone Poles*)

A185 "Deities and Beasts," *New Republic*, CXL (March 30, 1959), 17. (Collected in *Telephone Poles*)

A186 "Suburban Madrigal," *New Yorker*, XXXV (April 25, 1959), 200. (Collected in *Telephone Poles*)

A187 "In Praise of ($C_{10}H_9O_5$)," *New Yorker*, XXXV (May 16, 1959), 44. (Collected in *Telephone Poles*)

A188 "Sonic Boom," *New Yorker*, XXXV (August 8, 1959), 89. (Collected in *Telephone Poles*)

A189 "Tome-Thoughts, from the Times," *New Republic*, CXLI (August 10, 1959), 20. (Collected in *Telephone Poles*)

A190 "Fritillary," *New Yorker*, XXXV (August 15, 1959), 28. (Collected in *Telephone Poles*)

A191 "Thoughts While Driving Home," *New Yorker*, XXXV (September 26, 1959), 180. (Collected in *Telephone Poles*)

A192 "Idyll," *New Yorker*, XXXV (October 10, 1959), 50. (Collected in *Telephone Poles*)

A193 "Mobile of Birds," *New Yorker*, XXXV (December 19, 1959), 32. (Collected in *Telephone Poles*)

A194 "Yonder Peasant," *Contact*, IV (February, 1960), 52.

A195 "Martini," *Contact*, IV (February, 1960), 52.

A196 "Parable," *Contact*, IV (February, 1960), 53.

A197 "A Song of Paternal Care," *New Yorker*, XXXVI (March 19, 1960), 169. (Collected in *Telephone Poles*)

A198 "Modigliani's Death Mask," *New Yorker*, XXXVI (March 26, 1960), 34. (Collected in *Telephone Poles*)

A199 "Tropical Beetles," *New Yorker*, XXXVI (April 9, 1960), 154. (Collected in *Telephone Poles*)

A200 "B.W.I.," *New Yorker*, XXXVI (April 30, 1960), 98. (Collected in *Telephone Poles*)

A201 "Mosquito," *New Yorker*, XXXVI (June 11, 1960), 32. (Collected in *Telephone Poles*)

A202 "Meditation on a News Item," *New Yorker*, XXXVI (July 16, 1960), 38. (Collected in *Telephone Poles*)

A203 "Summer: Westside," *New Yorker*, XXXVI (July 30, 1960), 26. (Collected in *Telephone Poles*)

A204 "Agatha Christie and Beatrix Potter," *New Yorker*, XXXVI (November 26, 1960), 52. (Collected in *Telephone Poles*)

A205 "Wash," *New Yorker*, XXXVI (December 3, 1960), 161. (Collected in *Telephone Poles*)

A206 "Cosmic Gall," *New Yorker*, XXXVI (December 17, 1960), 36. (Collected in *Telephone Poles*)

A207 "Vision," *New Yorker*, XXXVI (January 7, 1961), 77.

A208 "Telephone Poles," *New Yorker*, XXXVI (January 21, 1961), 36. (Collected in *Telephone Poles*)

A209 "February 22," *New Yorker*, XXXVII (February 18, 1961), 40. (Collected in *Telephone Poles*)

A210 "Seven Stanzas at Easter," *Christian Century*, LXXVIII (February 22, 1961), 236. (Collected in *Telephone Poles*)

A211 "Comparative Religion," *New Yorker*, XXXVII (April 8, 1961), 51. (Collected in *Telephone Poles*)

A212 "Upon Learning That a Town Exists in Virginia Called Upperville," *New Yorker*, XXXVII (May 20, 1961), 135. (Collected in *Telephone Poles*)

A213 "Maples in a Spruce Forest," *Commonweal*, LXXIV (June 2, 1961), 252. (Collected in *Telephone Poles*)

A214 "Vermont," *Harper's*, CCXXIII (July, 1961), 67. (Collected in *Telephone Poles*)

A215 "I Missed His Book, But I Read His Name," *New Yorker*, XXXVII (November 4, 1961), 142. (Collected in *Telephone Poles*)

A216 "Old-Fashioned Lightning Rod," *New Yorker*, XXXVII (November 18, 1961), 171. (Collected in *Telephone Poles*)

A217 "Handkerchiefs of Khaiber Khan," *New Yorker*, XXXVII (November 25, 1961), 172.

A218 "Les Saints Nouveaux," *Harper's*, CCXXIV (January, 1962), 71. (Collected in *Telephone Poles*)

A219 "Stunt-Flier," *New Yorker*, XXXVII (January 6, 1962), 59. (Collected in *Telephone Poles*)

A220 "Marriage Counsel," *New Yorker*, XXXVII (January 20, 1962), 103. (Collected in *Telephone Poles*)

A221 "High-Hearts," *New Yorker*, XXXVIII (February 24, 1962), 30. (Collected in *Telephone Poles*)

A222 "Short Days," *New Yorker*, XXXVIII (March 10, 1962), 126. (Collected in *Telephone Poles*)

A223 "Earthworm," *New Yorker*, XXXVIII (May 12, 1962), 145. (Collected in *Telephone Poles*)

A224 "Die Neuen Heiliger," *Harper's*, CCXXV (August, 1962), 44. (Collected in *Telephone Poles*)

A225 "Seagulls," *New Yorker*, XXXVIII (August 25, 1962), 28. (Collected in *Telephone Poles*)

A226 "Calendar," *American Scholar*, XXXI (Autumn, 1962), 550. (Collected in *Telephone Poles*)

A227 "White Dwarf," *New Yorker*, XXXVIII (September 1, 1962), 67. (Collected in *Telephone Poles*)

A228 "Great Scarf of Birds," *New Yorker*, XXXVIII (October 27, 1962), 52. (Collected in *Telephone Poles*)

A229 "Flirt," *Commonweal*, LXXVII (November 30, 1962), 253. (Collected in *Telephone Poles*)

A230 "Bestiary," *New Yorker*, XXXVIII (December 1, 1962), 228. (Collected in *Telephone Poles*)

A231 "Exposure," *New Yorker*, XXXVIII (December 8, 1962), 49. (Collected in *Telephone Poles*)

A232 "Vibration," *New Yorker*, XXXIX (February 23, 1963), 30. (Collected in *Telephone Poles*)

A233 "Farewell to the Shopping District of Antibes," *New Yorker*, XXXIX (April 20, 1963), 50.

A234 "Hoeing," *New Yorker*, XXXIX (April 27, 1963), 142. (Collected in *Telephone Poles*)

A235 "Exposé," *New Yorker*, XXXIX (May 25, 1963), 40.

A236 "Erotic Epigrams," *Commonweal*, LXXVIII (June 14, 1963), 327. (Collected in *Telephone Poles*)

A237 "My Children at the Dump at Ipswich," *Transatlantic Review*, No. 14 (Autumn, 1963), 70.

A238 "Some Frenchmen," *New Yorker*, XXXIX (November 9, 1963), 54.

A239 "Azores," *Harper's*, CCXXVIII (January, 1964), 37.

A240 "Lamplight," *New Republic*, CL (February 29, 1964), 22.

A241 "Sea Knell," *New Yorker*, XL (March 28, 1964), 44.

A242 "Vow," *New Yorker*, XL (May 23, 1964), 48.

A243 "Fireworks," *New Yorker*, XL (July 4, 1964), 28.

A244 "Roman Portrait Busts," *New Republic*, CLII (February 6, 1965), 21.

A245 "Poem For a Far Land," *New Republic*, CLII (March 13, 1965), 17.

A246 "Sunshine on Sandstone," *New Republic*, CLII (April 17, 1965), 26.

A247 "Postcards from Soviet Cities: Moscow, Kiev, Leningrad, Yerevan," *New Yorker*, XLI (May 29, 1965), 34.

A248 "Décor," *American Scholar*, XXXIV (Summer, 1965), 412.

A249 "Home Movies," *New Republic*, CLIV (January 8, 1966), 23.

A250 "The Lament of Abzashka Tertz," *New Leader*, XLIX (January 17, 1966), 3.

A251 "Seal in Nature," *New Republic*, CLV (October 15, 1966), 16.

A252 "The Amish," *Saturday Review*, XLIX (October 22, 1966), 4.

A253 "Air Show," *New Republic*, CLV (December 17, 1966), 25.

A254 "Elm," *Polemic*, XI (Winter, 1966), 31.

A255 "Antigua," *New Yorker*, XLII (February 11, 1967), 46.

3. Periodicals: Short Fiction

A256 "The Different One," *Harvard Lampoon*, CXL (May, 1951), 12.

A257 Untitled, *Harvard Lampoon*, CXL (December 22, 1951), 14-15.

A258 "Summer of the Ivy," *Harvard Lampoon*, CXLI (May, 1952), 8-10.

A259 "Enlightenment," *Harvard Lampoon*, CXLI (November, 1952), 2-6.

A260 "The Enormous Package," *Harvard Lampoon*, CXLI (December, 1952), 18-21.

A261 "Alice the Timid Typhoon," *Harvard Lampoon,* CXLII (February, 1953), 10-11.

A262 "Dateline: Luna," *Harvard Lampoon*, CXLII (April, 1953), 2-4.

A263 "They Don't Play Bouffle Anymore," *Harvard Lampoon*, CXLII (April, 1953), 8-9.

A264 "Little Schism," *Harvard Lampoon*, CXLII (April, 1953), 17-24.

A265 "In Memoriam," *Harvard Lampoon*, CXLII (May, 1953), 12-13.

A266 "All for Society," *Harvard Lampoon*, CXLII (June, 1953), 8-10.

A267 "The New Generation," *Harvard Lampoon*, CXLII (September, 1953), 5.

A268 "She's a Very Cleanly Dog," *Harvard Lampoon*, CXLII (September, 1953), 11.

A269 "The Peruvian in the Heart of Lake Winnipesaukee," *Harvard Lampoon*, CXLII (September, 1953), 19-23.

A270 "The Sunshine Poet," *Harvard Lampoon*, CXLII (December, 1953), 8-11.

A271 "The Balanced Budget," *Harvard Lampoon*, CXLII (December, 1953), 22-24.

A272 "Supply is Unlimited," *Harvard Lampoon*, CXLII (February, 1954), 14-15.

A273 "Music for the Masses," *Harvard Lampoon*, CXLIII (February, 1954), 24.

A274 "Spring Comes to Cambridge," *Harvard Lampoon*, CXLIII (May, 1954), 14-21.

A275 "Hold Up," *Harvard Lampoon*, CXLIII (June, 1954), 19-23.

A276 "Friends from Philadelphia," *New Yorker*, XXX (October 30, 1954), 29-32. (Collected in *Same Door* and *Olinger Stories*)

A277 "Ace in the Hole," *New Yorker*, XXXI (April 9, 1955), 92-99. (Collected in *Same Door*)

A278 "Tomorrow and Tomorrow, Etc.," *New Yorker*, XXXI (April 30, 1955), 80. (Collected in *Same Door*)

A279 "Dentistry and Doubt," *New Yorker*, XXXI (October 29, 1955), 28-30. (Collected in *Same Door*)

A280 "Kid's Whistling," *New Yorker*, XXXI (December 3, 1955), 127-128. (Collected in *Same Door*)

A281 "Snowing in Greenwich Village," *New Yorker*, XXXI (January 21, 1956), 30-33. (Collected in *Same Door*)

A282 "Toward Evening," *New Yorker*, XXXI (February 11, 1956), 28-30. (Collected in *Same Door*)

A283 "Who Made the Yellow Roses Yellow?" *New Yorker*, XXXII (April 7, 1956), 28-34. (Collected in *Same Door*)

A284 "His Finest Hour," *New Yorker*, XXXII (June 23, 1956), 26-31. (Collected in *Same Door*)

A285 "Sunday Teasing," *New Yorker*, XXXII (October 13, 1956), 46-48. (Collected in *Same Door*)

A286 "A Trillion Feet of Gas," *New Yorker*, XXXII (December 8, 1956), 51-56. (Collected in *Same Door*)

A287 "Incest," *New Yorker*, XXXIII (June 29, 1957), 22-27. (Collected in *Same Door*)

A288 "The Alligators," *New Yorker*, XXXIV (March 22, 1958), 28-31. (Collected in *Same Door* and *Olinger Stories*)

A289 "Intercession," *New Yorker*, XXXIV (August 30, 1958), 24-27. (Collected in *Same Door*)

A290 "The Happiest I've Been," *New Yorker*, XXXIV (January 3, 1959), 24-31. Reprinted in *Stories from the New Yorker, 1950-1960*. New York: Simon and Schuster, 1960, pp. 152-166. (Collected in *Same Door* and *Olinger Stories*)

A291 "Still Life," *New Yorker*, XXXIV (January 24, 1959), 35-41. (Collected in *Pigeon Feathers*)

A292 "Vergil Moss," *New Yorker*, XXXV (April 11, 1959), 99-102.

A293 "Should Wizard Hit Mommy?" *New Yorker*, XXXV (June 13, 1959), 38-40. (Collected in *Pigeon Feathers*)

A294 "The Persistence of Desire," *New Yorker*, XXXV (July 11, 1959), 22-26. (Collected in *Pigeon Feathers* and *Olinger Stories*)

A295 "Flight," *New Yorker*, XXXV (August 22, 1959), 30-37. (Collected in *Pigeon Feathers* and *Olinger Stories*)

A296 "Dear Alexandros," *New Yorker*, XXXV (October 31, 1959), 40-41. (Collected in Pigeon Feathers)

A297 "Archangel," *Big Table*, II (No. 5, 1960), 78-79.

A298 "A Sense of Shelter," *New Yorker*, XXXV (January 16, 1960), 28-34. Reprinted in David Sohn, ed. *Ten Modern American Short Stories*. New York: Bantam, 1965, pp. 67-80. (Collected in *Pigeon Feathers* and *Olinger Stories*)

A299 "Wife-Wooing," *New Yorker*, XXXVI (March 12, 1960), 49-51. (Collected in *Pigeon Feathers*)

A300 "You'll Never Know, Dear, How Much I Love You," *New Yorker*, XXXVI (June 18, 1960), 39-40. (Collected in *Pigeon Feathers* and *Olinger Stories*)

A301 "Home," *New Yorker*, XXXVI (July 9, 1960), 26-31. (Collected in *Pigeon Feathers*)

A302 "The Doctor's Wife," *New Yorker*, XXXVI (February 11, 1961), 35-38. (Collected in *Pigeon Feathers*)

A303 "The Crow in the Woods," *Transatlantic Review*, No. 8 (Winter, 1961), 47-50. (Collected in *Pigeon Feathers*)

A304 "The Astronomer," *New Yorker*, XXXVII (April 1, 1961), 28-30. (Collected in *Pigeon Feathers*)

A305 "Lifeguard," *New Yorker*, XXXVII (June 17, 1961), 28-31. (Collected in *Pigeon Feathers*)

A306 "A & P," *New Yorker*, XXXVII (July 22, 1961), 22-24. Reprinted in James Moffett and Kenneth McElheny, eds. *Points of View*. New York: New American Library, 1966, pp. 204-210. (Collected in *Pigeon Feathers*)

A307 "Pigeon Feathers," *New Yorker*, XXXVII (August 19, 1961), 23-34. (Collected in *Pigeon Feathers* and *Olinger Stories*)

A308 "Packed Dirt, Churchgoing, A Dying Cat, A Traded Car," *New Yorker*, XXXVII (December 16, 1961), 59-62. (Collected in *Pigeon Feathers* and *Olinger Stories*)

A309 "Blessed Man of Boston, My Grandmother's Thimble, and Fanning Island," *New Yorker*, XXXVII (January 13, 1962), 28-33. (Collected in *Pigeon Feathers* and *Olinger Stories*)

A310 "Unstuck," *New Yorker*, XXXVII (February 3, 1962), 24-27.

A311 "In Football Season," *New Yorker*, XXXVIII (November 10, 1962), 48-49. (Collected in *Olinger Stories* and *Music School*)

A312 "A Madman," *New Yorker*, XXXVIII (December 22, 1962), 34-38. (Collected in *Music School*)

A313 "After the Storm," *Esquire*, LIX (January, 1963), 81. (Reprinted in Section II of *The Centaur*)

A314 "On the Way to School," *New Yorker*, XXXVIII (January 5, 1963), 32-40. (Reprinted in Section VIII of *The Centaur*)

A315 "Giving Blood," *New Yorker*, XXXIX (April 6, 1963), 36-41. (Collected in *Music School*)

A316 "The Indian," *New Yorker*, XXXIX (August 17, 1963), 24-26. (Collected in *Music School*)

A317 "At a Bar in Charlotte Amalie," *New Yorker*, XXXIX (January 11, 1964), 26-32. (Collected in *Music School*)

A318 "Twin Beds in Rome," *New Yorker*, XXXIX (February 8, 1964), 32-35. (Collected in *Music School*)

A319 "Christian Roommates," *New Yorker*, XL (April 4, 1964), 44-50. (Collected in *Music School*)

A320 "Lucid Eye in Silver Town," *Saturday Evening Post*, CCXXXVII (May 23, 1964), 54-55. (Collected in *Assorted Prose*)

A321 "The Morning," *New Yorker*, XL (July 18, 1964), 24-26. (Collected in *Music School*)

A322 "Dark," *New Yorker*, XL (October 31, 1964), 61-62. (Collected in *Music School*)

A323 "Leaves," *New Yorker*, XL (November 14, 1964), 52-53. (Collected in *Music School*)

A324 "Music School," *New Yorker*, XL (December 12, 1964), 50-52. (Collected in *Music School*)

A325 "Rescue," *New Yorker*, XL (January 2, 1965), 28-31. (Collected in *Music School*)

A326 "Hermit," *New Yorker*, XLI (February 20, 1965), 38-46. (Collected in *Music School*)

A327 "Bulgarian Poetess," *New Yorker*, XLI (March 13, 1965), 44-51. (Collected in *Music School*)

A328 "Stare," *New Yorker*, XLI (April 3, 1965), 41-43. (Collected in *Music School*)

A329 "Family Meadow," *New Yorker*, XLI (July 24, 1965), 24-25. (Collected in *Music School*)

A330 "My Lover Has Dirty Fingernails," *New Yorker*, XLI (July 17, 1965), 28-31. (Collected in *Music School*)

A331 "Deus Dixit," *Esquire*, LXIV (September, 1965), 100-102.

A332 "The Alligators," *Parents Magazine*, XL (September, 1965), 62-63. (See A288)

A333 "Four Sides of One Story," *New Yorker*, XLI (October 9, 1965), 48-52. (Collected in *Music School*)

A334 "Avec la Bébé-Sitter," *New Yorker*, XLI (January 1, 1966), 24-27. (Collected in *Music School*)

A335 "Marching Through Boston," *New Yorker*, XLI (January 22, 1966), 34-38. Reprinted in Wm. Abrahams, ed. *Prize Stories 1967: The O. Henry Awards.* New York: Doubleday & Co., 1967, pp. 105-114.

A336 "Harv Is Plowing Now," *New Yorker*, XLII (April 23, 1966), 46-48. (Collected in *Music School*)

A337 "Witnesses," *New Yorker*, XLII (August 13, 1966), 27-29.

A338 "Pro," *New Yorker*, XLII (September 17, 1966), 53-54.

A339 "Bech in Rumania," *New Yorker*, XLII (October 8, 1966), 54-63.

A340 "Your Lover Just Called," *Harper's*, CCXXXIV (January, 1967), 48-51.

A341 "Taste of Metal," *New Yorker*, XLIII (March 11, 1967), 49-51.

4. Periodicals: Reviews

A342 "Review in Reverse," *Harvard Lampoon*, CXLI (September, 1952), 14.

A343 "Nightmares and Daymares," *New York Times Book Review*, January 3, 1960, pp. 4, 22.

A344 "Poetry from Downtrodden," *New Republic*, CXLII (May 9, 1960), 11-12. (Collected in *Assorted Prose*)

A345 "Snow from a Dead Sky," *New Republic*, CXLIII (November 28, 1960), 26-27. (Collected in *Assorted Prose*)

A346 "Beerbohm and Others," *New Yorker*, XXXVII (September 16, 1961), 163-176. (Collected in *Assorted Prose*)

A347 "Anxious Days for the Glass Family," *New York Times Book Review*, September 17, 1961, pp.1, 52. Reprinted as "Franny and Zooey" in H. A. Grunwald, ed. *Salinger*. New York: Harper and Row, 1962, pp. 53-56. (Collected in *Assorted Prose* as "Franny and Zooey")

A348 "Creatures of the Air," *New Yorker*, XXXVII (September 30, 1961), 161-167. (Collected in *Assorted Prose*)

A349** "Briefly Noted," *New Yorker*, XXXVIII (March 24, 1962), 176, 178. (The review on p.176 is collected in *Assorted Prose*)

A350 "No Use Talking," *New Republic*, CXLVII (August 13, 1962), 23-24. (Collected in *Assorted Prose*)

A351 "Indignations of a Senior Citizen," *New York Times Book Review*, November 25, 1962, p.5. (Collected in *Assorted Prose*)

A352 "More Love in the Western World," *New Yorker*, XXXIX (August 24, 1963), 90-104. (Collected in *Assorted Prose*)

A353 "Between a Wedding and a Funeral," *New Yorker*, XXXIX (September 14, 1963), 192-194. (Collected in *Assorted Prose*)

A354 "Faith in Search of Understanding," *New Yorker*, XXXIX (October 12, 1963), 203-210. (Collected in *Assorted Prose*)

A355 "The Classics of Realism," *American Scholar*, XXXII (Autumn, 1963), 660-664. (Collected in *Assorted Prose*)

A356 "Rhyming Max," *New Yorker*, XL (March 7, 1964), 176-181. (Collected in *Assorted Prose*)

A357 "Grandmaster Nabokov," *New Republic*, CLII (September 26, 1964), 15-18. (Collected in *Assorted Prose*)

A358 "How How It Was," *New Yorker*, XXXIX (December 19, 1964), 165-166. (Collected in *Assorted Prose*)

A359 "Death's Heads," *New Yorker*, XLI (October 2, 1965), 216-228.

A360 "The Author as Librarian," *New Yorker*, XLI (October 30, 1965), 223-246.

A361 "The Fork," *New Yorker*, XLII (February 26, 1966), 115-134.

A362 "Mastery of Miss Warner," *New Republic*, CLIV (March 5, 1966), 23.

A363 "Mastery of Miss Warner," *Correction*, CLIV (March 26, 1966), 40. (This is the same review as that entered under A362)

A364 "Amoeba," *New Republic*, CLIV (June 25, 1966), 23.

A365 "Two Points on a Descending Curve," *New Yorker*, XLII (January 7, 1967), 91-94.

A366 "Nabokov's Look Back: A National Loss," *Life*, LXII (January 13, 1967), 9.

5. Periodicals: Articles

A367 "Portuguese for the Portuguese," *Harvard Lampoon*, CXLI (October, 1952), 2-7.

A368 "At the Pleasure XXXII," *Harvard Lampoon*, CXLII (April, 1953), 12.

A369 "The Better Third," *Harvard Lampoon*, CXLII (May, 1953), 20.

A370 "The Fading of the Fad," *Harvard Lampoon*, CXLII (October, 1953), 10-11.

A371 "The American Man: What of Him?" *New Yorker*, XXXII (January 12, 1957), 22. (Collected in *Assorted Prose*)

A372 "Notes," *New Yorker*, XXXII (January 26, 1957), 28-29.

A373 "Anywhere is Where You Hang Your Hat," *New Yorker*, XXXIII (June 8, 1957), 97-98. (Collected in *Assorted Prose*)

A374 "And Whose Little Generation Are You?" *New Yorker*, XXXIII (October 5, 1957), 38-39.

A375 "Outing," *New Yorker*, XXXIV (June 14, 1958), 28-29.

A376 "On the Sidewalk," *New Yorker*, XXXV (February 21, 1959), 32. (Collected in *Assorted Prose*)

A377 "Drinking from a Cup Made Cinchy," *New Yorker*, XXXV (March 21, 1959), 41-42. (Collected in *Assorted Prose*)

A378 "What is a Rhyme?" *Contact*, II (1959), 57-60. (Collected in *Assorted Prose*)

A379 "Confessions of a Wild Bore," *New Yorker*, XXXV (February 6, 1960), 34-35. (Collected in *Assorted Prose*)

A380 "The Sea's Green Sameness," *New World Writing*, No. 17 (1960), 54-59.

A381 "Hub Fans Bid Kid Adieu," *New Yorker*, XXXVI (October 22, 1960), 109-131. (Collected in *Assorted Prose*)

A382 "Why Robert Frost Should Receive the Nobel Prize," *Audience*, VII (Summer, 1960), 45-46. (Collected in *Assorted Prose*)

A383 "Unread Book Route," *New Yorker*, XXXVII (March 4, 1961), 28-29. (Collected in *Assorted Prose*)

A384 "Alphonse Peintre," *New Yorker*, XXXVII (March 18, 1961), 159-161. (Collected in *Assorted Prose*)

A385 "Mr. Ex-Resident," *New Yorker*, XXXVII (August 5, 1961), 27. Reprinted In Henry Carlisle's *American Satire in Prose and Verse*. New York: Random House, 1962, pp. 107-109. (Collected in *Assorted Prose*)

A386 "My Uncle's Death," *Saturday Evening Post*, CCXXXVI (March 2, 1963), 48-50. (Collected in *Assorted Prose*)

A387 "Eclipse," *Saturday Evening Post*, CCXXXVI (November 16, 1963), 92. (Collected in *Assorted Prose*)

A388 "Mea Culpa," *New Yorker*, XXXIX (November 16, 1963), 137-140. (Collected in *Assorted Prose*)

A389 "An Arion Questionnaire," *Arion*, III (Winter, 1964), 4.

A390 "Comment," *Times Literary Supplement*, June 4, 1964, p. 473.

B. Secondary Sources

1. Books

B1 Detweiler, Robert. "John Updike and the Indictment of Culture-Protestants." In his *Four Spiritual Crises in Mid-Century American Fiction*. Gainesville: University of Florida Press, 1963, pp.14-24.

> A lengthy and valuable discussion of *Rabbit, Run* and its attempt to expose a society condemned by Updike. Also, a close comparison to Niebuhr's theology, with quotes from the latter and from Updike.

B2 Finkelstein, Sidney. *Existentialism and Alienation in American Literature*. New York: International Publishers, 1965, pp.243-252.

> This pictures Updike as alienated, like Rabbit and Caldwell; a writer of a bleak world in a Nietzschean manner. Also, a discussion of *Rabbit, Run* and *Centaur*, not critical but analytical, as alienated expression and existential answer, respectively.

B3 Galloway, David. "The Absurd Man as Saint." In his *The Absurd Hero in American Fiction*. Austin: University of Texas Press, 1966, pp.21-50. (See B19)

> Perhaps the lengthiest—certainly most thorough—examination of *Poorhouse Fair*, the latter viewed as a foundation for the two absurd heroes who follow in *Centaur* and *Rabbit, Run*. *Poorhouse* discussed as a Utopian novel; Updike as an observer, yet quite involved. A discussion of Rabbit and Caldwell as Saints, with reference to many passages and to other writers of the absurd. An Updike checklist appears on pp.183-200.

31

B4 Hicks, Granville. "Generation of the 50's: Malamud, Gold, Updike." In Nona Balakian, ed. *The Creative Present.* Garden City: Doubleday, 1963, pp.217-237.

> A comparison of Malamud and Gold, with the least discussion of Updike; all three seen as seeking path for redemption. Updike's stories and first three novels are cited, with some biographical material.

B5 Mizener, Arthur. "The American Hero as High School Boy." In his *The Sense of Life in the Modern Novel.* Boston: Houghton Mifflin, 1964, pp.247-260.

> A careful study of Peter Caldwell (*Centaur*) and of Updike compared to Salinger. Discussion of a conflict between style and subject: latter as simple, former as ornate. Biographical sketch with likeness to McLeish; Updike as an American dilemma. An excellent article.

B6 O'Connor, William Van. "John Updike and William Styron." In Harry T. Moore, ed. *Contemporary American Novelists.* Carbondale: Southern Illinois University Press, 1964, pp.205-221.

> A valuable discussion of Updike's career as a novelist, with brief summaries and comments on the first three novels. Updike is seen as having more theme and more language than Styron, thus more chance of success. Central characters and central questions are discussed.

B7 Peden, William. *The American Short Story: Front Line in the National Defense of Literature.* Boston: Houghton Mifflin, 1964, pp.68-72.

> A discussion of Updike's characters, their "Middle" qualities resulting in stories without catastrophe yet with tragedy in the commonplace. Updike's capacity for beautifying the little is illustrated. Updike is pictured as a "frightening talent."

B8 Podhoretz, Norman. "A Dissent on Updike." In his *Doings and Undoings.* New York: Farrar, Straus, 1964, pp.251-257. (See B234)

> A sharp dissent, suggesting that Updike is unimaginative,

unconvincing in characterization, adolescent in sexual attitudes. Updike is discussed as having nothing to say, as an average writer.

B9 Welker, Robert. *The Sense of Fiction.* Englewood, N.J.: Prentice-Hall, 1966, pp.44-47.

Updike's story "A Sense of Shelter" is included in a text book format with comments and a "study guide." A not very scholarly, but interesting, study of Updike as a realist; compared to Poe.

2. Periodical Articles

B10 Brenner, Gerry. "John Updike's Criticism of the Return to Nature," *Twentieth Century Literature*, XII (April, 1966), 3-14.

> This is perhaps the best study of Updike and of *Rabbit,Run* in particular; the 20th century noble, urban savage whose sense of duty is aroused only by natural events. Updike is pictured as a philosophical conservative.

B11 Burgess, Anthony. "Language, Myth, and Mr. Updike," *Commonweal*, LXXXIII (February 11, 1966), 557-559.

> A European view of Updike as the "ghost of Henry James"; a concern for both European style and American energy, with comments on and comparison of three latest novels.

B12 De Bellis, Jack. "The Group and John Updike," *Sewanee Review*, LXXII (Summer, 1964), 531-536.

> An analysis of Updike as a successful illustrator of the modern conflict between desire for love and the necessity of self-knowledge. Also, comments on *Same Door* stories; these considered superior to the novels.

B13 Davenport, Guy. "Magic Realism in Prose," *National Review*, XIII (August 28, 1962), 153-154.

> There is not much on Updike here, merely his inclusion in a school of "Modern Realism" with Bellow, Roth, Baldwin and Gold (whose works are reviewed here): a school of "enamaled prose and exact observation."

B14 "Desperate Weakling," *Time*, LXXVI (November 7, 1960), 108.

> Partial review of *Rabbit,Run*, but more a comment on Updike and his background. Rabbit's decision to run is seen as indicative that man now lets loose from quiet desperation.

B15* Doner, Dean. "Rabbit Angstrom's Unseen World," *New World Writing*, No. 19 (1961), 58-75.

B16 Doyle, Paul. "Updike's Fiction: Motifs and Techniques," *Catholic World*, LXLIX (September, 1964), 356-362.
A significant defense of Updike as an artist with a serious message, supported by presentation of questions concerning morality and religion. Some comparison to Salinger is included.

B17 Duncan, Graham. "The Thing Itself in *Rabbit,Run,*" *English Record*, XIII (April, 1963), 36-37.
A discussion of Updike's two egos: the self and the concept of writer. Updike seen as Rabbit in a search for an essence. This is part of a longer essay read to the New York State English Council.

B18 Enright, D. J. "Updike's Ups and Downs," *Holiday*, XXXVIII (November, 1965), 162-166.
Rather sharp criticism drawing from each novel suggesting that Updike is a nature poet with little to say; interrelated themes as the only characteristics of a major writer.

B19 Galloway, David. "The Absurd Hero in Contemporary American Fiction," *Dissertation Abstracts*, XXIII (April, 1963), 4356-4357 (Buffalo). (See B3)
A study of the works of Updike, Styron, Bellow and Salinger, each as having studied absurdity thoroughly. The discussion is based upon Camus' myth of the absurd; more general than directed to Updike.

B20 Galloway, David. "The Absurd Man as Saint," *Modern Fiction Studies*, X (Summer, 1964), 111-127. (See B3)
A rather comprehensive study of three first novels, showing Updike's use of characters to illustrate man's quest and eventual superiority over the absurd, his discussion of Christianity and Humanism.

B21 Geismar, Maxwell. "The American Short Story Today," *Studies on the Left*, IV (Spring, 1964), 21-27.
A discussion of Updike's short stories as ineffectual; Updike

discussed with Salinger, Roth, Malamud, Grau, etc., with a brief comment on *The Centaur*, but little of significance.

B22 Geller, Evelyn. "WLB Biography," *Wilson Library Bulletin*, XXXVI (September, 1961), 67.

A lengthy biographical sketch with comments on all published work until 1961; reference to and quotes from various critics.

B23 Hamilton, Kenneth. "John Updike: Chronicler of the Time of the 'Death of God,'" *Christian Century*, LXXXIV (June 7, 1967), 745-748.

An excellent discussion of Updike's theological literacy, this article covers several short stories and all the novels, each related to 20th century boredom and de-spiritualization.

B24 Hathaway, Baxter. "Reviewers as Sleepwalkers," *Epoch*, XIV (Winter, 1965), 188-192.

This essay is on book reviewers, with insignificant comment on Updike; merely the claim that he equates intellect with excellence in basketball.

B25 Kauffman, Stanley. "Onward With Updike," *New Republic*, CLV (September 24, 1966), 15-17.

An analysis of Updike as one who believes that large meanings do not always come from large events; his concept of love as a religious belief, with brief notes on specific works and on Updike as a novelist. This is original and helpful.

B26 Klausler, A. P. "Steel Wilderness," *Christian Century*, LXXVIII (February 22, 1961), 245-246.

A rather comprehensive study of themes based upon the Christian ethic, with brief biographical sketch, discussion of *Poorhouse* and *Rabbit,Run*, and the suggestion of Updike as a prophetic voice.

B27 La Course, Guerin. "The Innocence of John Updike," *Commonweal*, LXXVII (December 7, 1962), 512-514.

This discussion of Updike's ability to reflect upon youthful innocence and the quest for love as a dominant theme. The claim is made that only a loss of innocence will assume him the stance of major novelist. Discussion of *Poorhouse* and *Rabbit,Run* adds to this significant study.

B28 Mailer, Norman. "Norman Mailer vs. Nine Writers," *Esquire*, LX (July, 1963), 63-69, 105.

A sharp criticism with little support, some of which comes from *Rabbit,Run*. An emotionally-charged claim that Updike is good but never great; this is not for scholarly tastes.

B29 Muradian, Thaddeus. "The World of John Updike," *English Journal*, LIV (October, 1965), 577-584.

A lengthy and original discussion of four areas forming a motif: childhood, pain and loneliness, death, hope. Many illustrations with a conclusion of a Christian-Judaic view: salvation through a way of life. This is quite helpful in relation to most work.

B30 Novak, Michael. "Updike's Quest for Liturgy," *Commonweal*, LXXVII (May 10, 1963), 192-195.

This is an interesting criticism of critics of Updike, with skillful discussion of four stories: "Packed Dirt," "Churchgoing," "A Dying Cat," "A Traded Car," illustrates what Updike is saying and what critics fail to hear. A claim that Updike is trying to make religion intelligible in America concludes an excellent essay.

B31 "Run from Rabbit," *America*, CIV (November 19, 1960), 257.

An emotional editorial condemning critics who find merit in Updike's style. His work is discussed as restless and all-pervading.

B32 Schwartz, Jonathan. "Updike of Ipswich," *Boston*, (August, 1965), 35.

An interesting character sketch, with a suggestion of candor, humility, accessibility; notes on geography and on family, and a comparison to Salinger, with brief comments on some work.

B33 Serebuick, Judith. "New Creative Writers," *Library Journal*, LXXXIV (February 1, 1959), 499.

Mostly quoting directly from Updike, there are interesting

insights through these recorded talks, with comments on *Poorhouse*.

B34 Stern, Richard. "The Myth in Action," *Spectator*, No. 7057 (September 27, 1963), 389.

> A sketchy discussion of *Centaur* and *Rabbit,Run*, but an original comparison to John O'Hara. Also reference to *Poorhouse* and *Pigeon Feathers*.

B35 Sullivan, Walter. "Updike, Spark, and Others," *Sewanee Review*, LXXIV (Summer, 1966), 709-716.

> A brief discussion of Updike's background and of the autobiographical references in certain work; an interesting capsule of *Assorted Prose*, *Of The Farm* and *Rabbit,Run*, though no deep analysis.

B36 "Sustaining Stream," *Time*, LXXXI (February 1, 1963), M24, M26.

> This rather superficial coverage of several writers, including Updike's later career reviewed as in general literary opinion, has little new to say.

B37 Tate, Sister M. Judith. "Of Rabbits and Centaurs," *Critic*, XXII (February-March, 1964), 44-47, 49-50.

> A rather detailed—certainly original—discussion of the two novels as allegory. Characters are analyzed from a theological view, related to Buber's "I-Thou" concept, though the latter is not cited.

B38* Waldmeir, Joseph. "Accommodations in the New Novel," *University College Quarterly*, XI (November, 1965), 26-32.

B39 Ward, John A. "John Updike's Fiction," *Critique*, V (Spring-Summer, 1962), 27-41.

> A general praise for craft but the claim is made that *New Yorker* is a bad influence, stifles theme. The lengthy discussion of *Rabbit,Run*—interestingly considered unworkable—is helpful. Citation of other critics is included.

B40 Yates, Norris. "The Doubt and Faith of John Updike," *College English*, XXVI (March, 1965), 469-474.

An examination of the religious undercurrent in much of Updike's work, based upon the thesis that Updike shares Unamuno's tragic sense of life. This interesting relation of author's life to work and characters shows Updike as neither secular nor sectarian. Three first novels and several short stories are discussed at length.

3. Reviews

The Carpentered Hen

B41 *Booklist*, LIV (April 15, 1958), 470.
> A brief account of recurring themes and praise for "skill, variety, and comic sense . . . a serious undercurrent" in Updike's work.

B42 *Bookmark*, XVII (April, 1958), 169.
> This mere sentence of description suggests that the work "nicely blends content and wit."

B43 Denver, Colo. *Post*, April 27, 1958, Roundup Sec., p.12.
> A very brief description of this collection as light, not to be worked over, yet with "depths and tenderness as well as the more marketable brass."

B44 Dorn, Norman. "An English Accent is Heard in the New Modern Poetry," San Francisco *Chronicle*, November 23, 1958, p.13.
> Hardly valuable, this very brief description includes one example of the work.

B45 *Kirkus*, XXVI (January 15, 1958), 59.
> A list of the types of poems, but no direct reference, with verse said to display "a bent for word usage, the exercise of ideas, spontaneity, and a pleasant type of ingenuity."

B46 McCord, David. *Saturday Review*, XLI (August 9, 1958), 32.
> The claim is made that "trivia of life" is Updike's main source of material. Notes on a few poems suggest that Updike has developed "a maturity of technique."

B47 McDonald, G. *Library Journal*, LXXXIII (June 15, 1958), 1938.

With a very brief note on poems of "amiable deflation," Mc-
Donald suggests that "Updike develops a poem that is witty,
elegant, and inventive."

The Poorhouse Fair

B48 Adams, Phoebe. *Atlantic*, CCIII (February, 1959), 100.
This brief, superficial review suggests the novel as "a study of
the survival of spiritual vitality in a most unlikely setting."

B49 *America*, C (January 31, 1959), 528.
A brief description and sketchy analysis of the novel as "an
elegantly wrought little gem"; compares the work to Welty's
"The Ponder Heart."

B50* *Apostalic Perspectives*, IV (March, 1959), 31.

B51 "As They Wait to Die," *Newsweek*, LIII (January 12,
1959), 90.
With praise for and summary of novel, the editors suggest
"Updike never lets us forget that the misunderstandings arise
from significant differences in basic values."

B52 Balliett, Whitney. "Writer's Writer," *New Yorker*,
XXXIV (February 7, 1959), 138-142.
A lengthy, interesting, and quite favorable discussion of Updike as a poetic novelist, in the ranks of Welty and Nabokov:
"poetic vision, tied loosely to earth only by its outward form
of narrative prose." This valuable review suggests that the
tale is macabre without sentimentality.

B53 Barr, Donald. "A Stone's Throw Apart," *New York
Times Book Review*, January 11, 1959, p.4.
The novel is praised as philosophical, theological, with a summary of plot and description of character offered: ". . . moves
us by its microscopic clarity . . . the conflict of real ideals, of
real personalities."

B54 Betts, Doris. "Fine Novel by Updike," *Virginian Pilot*,
January 25, 1959, p.6F.
Approval is given here of careful detail and characterization,

but dissent for failure to examine philosophical themes. "Updike's talent with words is matched by his ability to think and to convey his thought."

B55 *Booklist*, LV (January 15, 1959), 260.

A brief, superficial review of the novel as one which "throws telling, indirect glances at the conflict between youth and age."

B56 *Bookmark*, XVIII (February, 1959), 121.

This is a hardly significant note of description.

B57 Buchanan, Leigh. *Epoch*, IX (Spring, 1959), 252-254.

An interesting comparison to Huxley's *Brave New World*, this analysis suggests novel "in terms of complicated imagery and metaphor of an imagined America of 15 years from now." The weakness in dramatization of abstractions is pointed out.

B58 Butcher, Fanny. "First Novel Talented, Tho Haphazard," Chicago *Sunday Tribune*, January 11, 1959, Pt.IV, p.4.

A short summary, with a description of the novel as "a literary mirror . . in which are [sic] reflected mood, character, sentiment, and implied philosophy as each incident evolves."

B59 Chase, Mary Ellen. "John Updike's Wise, Moving First Novel," *New York Herald Tribune Book Review*, January 11, 1959, p.3.

This description of setting and theme offers high praise for being "brilliant in design and language."

B60 Coleman, John. "Various Formalities," *Spectator*, No. 6820 (March 13, 1959), 380.

This is a very short description of "marvellously vivid and round characters."

B61 Diebold, Michael. "Updike Outwits Himself," Pittsburgh *Press*, January 11, 1959, Sec.3, p.6.

With a suggestion of theme and plot, the suggestion is offered of failure in Updike's "unaccountable decision to set his story in some indeterminate time of the future."

B62 "Do-Gooder Undone," *Time*, LXXIII (January 19, 1959), 92.

The editors here make claim of Updike's failure in refusing to talk of the "sin of Pride" in a novel which illustrates "the clash between the bloodless ideal of social perfectability and . . the old Adam."

B63 Fitelson, David. "Conflict Unresolved," *Commentary*, XXVII (March 3, 1959), 275-276.

A rapid summary of plot and theme lays Updike's failure to *New Yorker*: "a rather mannered way of exploring character, and a distaste for the sight of blood daintiness that he shares with certain other *New Yorker* contributors."

B64 Gilman, Richard. "A Last Assertion of Personal Being," *Commonweal*, LXIX (February 6, 1959), 499.

A rather rhetorical review of the novel as eloquent, with a good summary of action and discussion of philosophy, this is one of the best on this novel. Updike "sees, hears before he judges or constructs; his prose aims at the immaculate immediacy of things perceived."

B65 Grauel, Gerald. *Best Sellers*, XVIII (January 15, 1959), 400.

This brief summary of characters and activity includes an interesting note on work as "novelette in the field of gerontology."

B66* Hanscom, Leslie. New York *World Telegram and Sun*, January 14, 1959, p.31.

B67 Hester, Sister Mary. *Critic*, XVII (March, 1959), 39.

The summary suggests failure in that Updike "explores the possibilities of development of character . . . through descriptive blocks, tangental stream of consciousness and montage of dialogue."

B68 Hicks, Granville. "Novels in Limbo," *Saturday Review*, XLII (January 17, 1959), 58-59.

Though hope for future work is expressed there is little comment on this novel, merely that it is "deliberately and even self-consciously off-beat."

B69 Holzhauer, Jean. "Updike's Respect for Human Dignity," *Catholic Messanger*, (February 5, 1959).

With the novel summarized but not carefully analyzed, there is emphasis upon characterization. "Updike never interprets his elderly and failing characters as merely pitiful."

B70 Hughes, Riley. *Catholic World*, CLXXX (May, 1959), 162.

This sketchy review suggests that the novel is "a microcosm which reflects the issues and tensions of a larger world outside."

B71 Hutchens, John. "Poorhouse Fair," New York *Herald Tribune*, January 16, 1959, p.38.

This is a good capsule of the novel, with high praise for a youthful writer's ability to observe the elderly. "They (the old folks) speak for the individual's right to remain an individual, however wretched, in the face of doctrinaire authority ...."

B72 Irwin, Joan. *Tamarack Review*, (Spring, 1959), 102.

Irwin is rather critical, offering an outline of major plot and a description of the "overpowering setting (which) interrupts the mind and distracts the eye again and again."

B73 Johnson, J. H. *New Statesman*, LVII (March 28, 1959), 453.

This is a brief and very critical dismissal of the novel as "an attempt to get away from the great American terror of the Familiar."

B74 Joysmith, Toby. Mexico City *News*, April 5, 1959.

An original analysis of characters and plot, this review suggests an analogy of elderly to youthful of the Garden of Eden: "Man, growing older, makes his own explosion in this other garden of old age."

B75 *Kirkus*, XXVI (November 1, 1958), 830.

With a summary of theme and plot is the observation of Updike's "ability for portraying ... not only a place ... but also the quality of age and its relinquishing, reluctantly, to the past."

B76* Kohler, Dayton. Richmond, Va. *News Leader*, April 15, 1959.

B77 "Lots of Goodies, and Already, Yet," Washington *Post*, January 11, 1959, p.E7.

> A very brief summary with rather superficial comments on this "lyrical" novel: "Updike writes with the tongue of angels and sees with the eyes of a bird."

B78 Marchand, B. G. *Commonweal*, LXIX (February 27, 1959), 581.

> A high, but short, praise of this novel, considered here first of its kind since Cozzen's *By Love Possessed*: "Updike catches a slice of life through the wavering prism of old age, poverty and frustration."

B79 O'Leary, Ted. "Satires on the Welfare State," Kansas City *Star*, January 24, 1959, p.6.

> This brief summary, warning Updike to stay away from pseudo-intellectuals, is not helpful.

B80 Podhoretz, Norman. "Style and Substance," *Reporter*, XX (January 22, 1959), 42-44.

> This is a rather critical dissent on Updike as not giving a "stand," or posing serious problems; his work as having "absence of genuine conflict."

B81 Price, Martin. "Intelligence and Fiction: Some New Novels," *Yale Review*, XLVIII (March, 1959), 451-464.

> A discussion, though not too specific, of the novel as symbolic, claiming that Updike fails to have characters sustain any principle. Yet, the poorhouse is described as "a small, closed world within which a moral situation is defined."

B82 Rorty, James. "Life Among the Aged," *New Leader*, LXII (March 23, 1959), 25.

> Mostly summary of plot with much dialogue—perhaps the most significant—excerpted: "a philosophical discussion of life beyond the grave." Also, a comparison to the clear, "unsentimental" painting of Geo. Bellows.

B83 Salmon, Peter. "A Slice of Life," *New Republic*, CXL (January 12, 1959), 20.

> There is more here on publishing practices than on Updike,

with only a brief account of plot: "The book's strength lies in its many carefully developed and skillfully wrought pieces."

B84 Serebuick, Judith. *Library Journal*, LXXXIV (January 1, 1959), 123.

This is a quick summary of plot and themes: "much to say on individualism and conformity, mechanization and craftsmanship, the 'welfare state' and the 'old days'."

B85 Sherman, Thomas. "Reading and Writing," St. Louis, Mo. *Post-Dispatch*, March 1, 1959, p.4B.

High praise here and rather careful summary and description of characters and philosophy. "Updike pays tribute to the life force and a memorable commentary on what human beings value."

B86 "Ways of the World," *Times Literary Supplement*, March 20, 1959, p.157.

A brief summary of action and theme, and praise of the novel as "truthful, perceptive and coloured by a spirit of sad, unillusioned comedy, perfectly in keeping with the subject of old age."

The Same Door

B87 *Best Sellers*, XIX (September 1, 1959), 178.

This is a descriptive review, mostly from the point of view of style: ". . . sensitive fusing of tempo and tone, the perceptive character delineations, the deft plumbing of shallow existence.

B88 *Booklist*, LVI (September 1, 1959), 30.

A sketchy description citing themes, with little comment other than "sophisticated."

B89 *Bookmark*, XIX (October, 1959), 14.

Again, a quick note of description suggesting themes by noting "interplay of personality" in stories.

B90 Cassiday, T. E. "The Enchantment of the Ordinary," *Commonweal*, LXX (September 11, 1959), 499.

Updike is discussed here as craftsman; praise and comment

given on several stories: his "wonder at the beauty in the simple strangeness of things . . . delicately startling and imaginative."

B91 "Cool, Cool World," *Time*, LXXIV (August 17, 1959), 98.

This is a superficial review, with reference to three stories, suggesting Updike's "sense of the fashions of the times."

B92 Crane, Milton. "Young People With Time to Explore Their Souls," Chicago *Sunday Tribune*, August 16, 1959, Pt.IV, p.3.

Although a short description with patterns of themes only outlined, Crane's developing criticism is noteworthy. "Updike's art is essentially one of nuance and chiaroscuro . . . restrained poetic eloquence."

B93 "First Steps of Involvement," *Christian Science Monitor*, August 20, 1959, p.11.

A description of contents, with reference to several stories, the latter said to express "the conventional view of life," from point of view of "ironical detachment."

B94 Flory, Claude, *English Journal*, XLIX (February, 1960), 143.

This is brief praise of that work which reveals Updike's "attitude of affirmation without intrusive moralizing and . . . his talent for perfection of phrasing."

B95 "Fragments of America," *Times Literary Supplement*, April 27, 1962, p.277.

In this discussion of the stories as a reflection of American society, both strengths and weaknesses are suggested to lie in Updike's "investing of the insignificant episode with significance," his success upon "catching of the exact nuances of American scene and dialogue."

B96 Healey, R. C. "John Updike With a Packet of Stories," *New York Herald Tribune Book Review*, August 16, 1959, p.3.

This discussion in relation to *Poorhouse* suggests Updike's intention with reference to stories: "His characters are groping to find the same door of communication and understanding."

B97 Hutchens, John. "Same Door," New York *Herald Tribune*, August 17, 1959, p.13.

This description of contents makes a comparison to *Poorhouse*: "he is looking no less perceptively into the mind of the relatively young."

B98 Keown, Eric. *Punch*, CCXLII (May 2, 1962), 697.

A brief comment illustrating that "one learns a lot from these stories about the ordinary American scene."

B99* Kohler, Dayton. Richmond, Va. *News Leader*, September 9, 1959.

B100 Lodge, David. "Instant Novel," *Spectator*, No. 6985 (May 11, 1962), 628.

Stories are here again discussed as reflections of the American way of life, its "absurdities and ironies." Also a comparison to Joyce and praise for the collection as novelistic in its "ability to communicate the quality of a whole life in a few pages."

B101 Mayne, Richard. "Instant Literature," *New Statesman*, LXIII (April 27, 1962), 606.

There is not much reference to stories, but criticism of the collective character: "well-tailored, so impeccably right, emotionally so metrical": Mayne is haunted by a feeling of "déja vu."

B102 Peden, William. "Minor Ills That Plague the Human Heart," *New York Times Book Review*, August 16, 1959, p.5.

This summary of themes and reference to several stories suggest that characters are "plagued by all the ills that in the world of the 20th century intellectual have apparently replaced the medieval devil."

B103 Schott, Webster. "The 'Better' and the 'Best,' " Kansas City *Star*, August 29, 1959, p.6.

This description of stories suggests Updike as being "alert to the qualities of the times . . . finds pathos in the vicissitudes of life."

B104 Serebuick, Judith. *Library Journal*, LXXXIV (August, 1959), 2376.

This reference to a few stories includes illustration of a typical Updike character: "a young man . . . quiet, perceptive, somewhat uncertain of himself and his surroundings."

B105 Spectorsky, A. C. "Spirit Under Surgery," *Saturday Review*, XLII (August 22, 1959), 15.

There is not much reference to stories but there is much to style: Updike as "surgeon-poet of the spirit," as a sympathetic observer of "slices of life." Also, an interesting, fresh note on title of the book deriving from the superstition that one should enter and leave a house by the same door.

B106 Steggert, Francis. *Critic*, XVIII (November, 1959), 30.

Merely a general description of contents: "insights are clearly autobiographical, they naturally focus upon the experiences of youth and early adulthood."

B107 Tindall, Gillian. "Short Shift," *Time and Tide*, XLIII (April 26, 1962), 30.

Suggestive note on Updike as writing of life: "He has a remarkable talent for creating—or perceiving—a unity in things on different levels." A comparison to Salinger.

B108 *Virginia Quarterly Review*, XXXVI (Winter, 1960), xi-xii.

No stories are cited here; merely the observation that the "interest is in the reactions of the characters to some specfiic situation . . . that may hold a personal or emotional significance."

B109 "The World of Neon," *Newsweek*, LIV (August 17, 1959), 97.

A short examination, though much quotation, of stories as illuminating "those favorite fictional areas, New York and Suburbia."

B110 Yudkin, Vivian. "More Updike, More Magic," Washington *Post*, August 16, 1959, p.E7.

A brief description of stories as holding "a clever, thin balance between what *is* and what is felt."

Rabbit, Run

B111 Balliett, Whitney. "The American Expression," *New Yorker*, XXXVI (November 5, 1960), 222.
    Updike is discussed here as Mr. Average American, as writing for himself alone, trying to achieve "hyper-expression," and as detesting humankind "because it has not yet met his standards, which are part aesthetic, part moral."

B112 *Booklist*, LVII (November 15, 1960), 180.
    This is a brief summary of Rabbit's action, but with no careful conclusion.

B113 Boroff, David. "You Can't Really Flee," *New York Times Book Review*, November 6, 1960, p.4.
    A study of characterization, with summary and excerpts; the conclusion here is that the novel is "a tender and discerning study of the desparate and the hungering in our midst."

B114 Crane, Milton. "Rabbit Runs, But Can't Get Away From Himself," Chicago *Sunday Tribune*, November 13, 1960, Pt. IV, p.6.
    A brief and rather critical description: "the author fails to convince us that his puppets are interesting in themselves or that their plight has implications that transcend their narrow worlds."

B115 Crosby, John. "Novel of the 60's," New York *Herald Tribune*, December 23, 1960, p.17.
    This brief summary, with offense taken at use of sex, concludes that "There is a hopeless, helpless, vegetable philosophy here."

B116 Culligan, Glendy. Washington *Post*, November 13, 1960, p.E6.
    A brief description including a comparison to Paul Goodman's *Growing Up Absurd*: "Updike is too deft a writer to preach a sermon."

B117 Cunningham, Robert. *Best Sellers*, XX (November 15, 1960), 318.

> A brief but thorough summary of the plot, with the conclusion that Updike writes an "arresting, disturbing novel about life in America today," and with Rabbit discussed as a sympathetic character.

B118 "Desperate Weakling," *Time*, LXXVI (November 7, 1960), 108.

> An unusually good, lengthy discussion and summary seeing Updike as anchoring "Thoreau's belief that most men lead lives of quiet desperation," and critical of poor taste in the use of sex.

B119 Diebold, Michael. "Rabbit Runs As Net Tightens," Pittsburgh *Press*, November 11, 1960, p.9.

> This summary and description, with a slight comparison to *Poorhouse*, concludes that Updike is trying "to convey the misery and panic of a free spirit trapped by its own lust and dumb unluck in dishelved reality."

B120 Edelstein, J. M. "Down With the Poor in Spirit," *New Republic*, CXLIII (November 21, 1960), 17.

> A sociological study, this criticizes Updike for his lack of compassion: "Rabbit seems to represent the young American whose beliefs have no morality and whose manliness is limited to being able to perform the act which may reproduce himself."

B121 "Enemies of Promise," *Times Literary Supplement*, September 29, 1961, p.648.

> The novel is discussed here as a reflection of American society, with summary, and with the conclusion that Updike describes the "anti-climax of adult life after a great athletic success."

B122 Evans, Fallon. *Critic*, XIX (January, 1961), 63.

> A short but quite strong criticism of the novel as "terrible . . . Updike's real stock in trade is pitiless objectivity."

B123 Foster, Richard. "What is Fiction For?" *Hudson Review*, XIV (Spring, 1961), 142-149.

Treated briefly, along with seven other novelists, Updike is compared to Nathanael West; the novel is "an absorbing, serious, painful, beautiful rendering of man's self-entrapment."

B124 Fremont-Smith, Eliot. *Village Voice*, February 2, 1961, p.5.

A lucid, rather significant summary and analysis of plot and "anti-hero"; an interesting justification of Rabbit's lust, "his only real evidence of existence," and Updike as an "athlete of words and images."

B125* Galloway, David. *Night Watch*, I (May, 1961), 20.

B126 Gilman, Richard. "A Distinguished Image of Precarious Life," *Commonweal*, LXXIII (October 28, 1960), 128-129.

The novel is discussed as a "minor epic," as compared to the French, a branch of philosophy. Updike is discussed as "presenting us with a vision of what persists beneath the adjustments we have made to necessity." This is quite good.

B127 Gorn, L. H. "Three Novelists View Today's Times With Despair," San Francisco *Chronicle*, November 20, 1961, p.28.

This is a very short suggestion that Rabbit "continually scampers for cover—a cover elusive because non-existent."

B128 Hardwick, Elizabeth. *Harper's*, CCXXII (January, 1961), 104.

The novel is discussed as one of the "new, frank novels," but less successful than *Poorhouse*, less life-like: "pre-eminently lyrical and tender and also disillusioned."

B129 Hicks, Granville. "A Little Good in Evil," *Saturday Review*, XLIII (November 5, 1960), 28.

An interesting prediction of Updike's future promise, and the claim that he "is not merely compassionate; he has so deep a sense of human fallibility that he treasures the goodness . . . he finds in Rabbit."

B130 Hutchens, John. "Rabbit,Run," New York *Herald Tribune*, November 3, 1960, p.25.

This careful description of Rabbit as "part angel, part demon . . . Everyman in a drab world he never made" is critical of Updike for failure to "speak up."

B131 Kronman, Ruth. *National Guardian*, (February 27, 1961).

A brief analysis with emphasis upon Rabbit as protagonist. The conclusion here is that Updike has compassion, that "he examines this selfish, shallow, lustful creature and says: Feel for him."

B132 Lyons, R. "A High E. Q.," *Minnesota Review*, I (Spring, 1961), 385-389.

This discussion of Rabbit views his escape as a positive act, one of release, not unlike that of the artist; not a spineless act. Updike is pictured as misunderstood.

B133 Manning, Olivia. "Faces of Violence," *Spectator*, No. 6951 (September 15, 1961), 361.

A short description of the novel as less successful than *Poorhouse*: "the book resounds with a depressing emptiness."

B134* Massey, Inton. "Doomed Marriage Has Moral Aspects," Richmond, Va. *News Leader*, November 23, 1960.

B135 McGuinness, Frank. "In Extremis," *New Statesman*, LXII (September 29, 1961), 439.

This quick dismissal sees the novel as "a wearying round of introspective brooding and interminable sex."

B136* McLaughlin, Richard. Springfield *Republican*, November 20, 1960, p.5D.

B137 Miller, Norman. "Three of the Best," *Antioch Review*, XXI (Spring, 1961), 118-128.

This is a lengthy summary but brief analysis of *Rabbit,Run* related to other work; also a comparison to Holden Caulfield and Willy Loman.

B138 "A Novelist Gets Tough," *Newsweek*, LVI (November 7, 1960), 122.

A sketchy discussion of the novel as a story of the typical

American boy: "shallowness of the provincial, lower-middle-class mind has probably not been so brutally attacked since Flaubert."

B139 O'Leary, Ted. "Satisfying Life Eludes a Runner," Kansas City *Star*, November 5, 1960, p.6.

This rather good summary suggests that Rabbit is running "to find the quality that is missing from his life." Also, a discussion of Updike in general, as "so sensitive a person that he is affected intensely by everything which he experiences."

B140 *Playboy*, VIII (February, 1961), 34-35.

An oversimplified account, critical of Updike, and contrary to most criticism in praise of his perception, his detail.

B141 Price, R. G. G. *Punch*, CCXLI (September 20, 1961), 443.

A superficial comment suggesting the novel as one of pity; the sexual detail is stressed.

B142 Reif, Jane. "Unattractive Characters Get Pity," *Virginian Pilot*, January 1, 1961, p.7B.

This summary of plot, with mixed views, sees the work as "brilliant in its use of language, brilliant in its terrible awareness of every thought, every action of its people."

B143 Rugoff, Milton. "American Tragedy, 1960," *New York Herald Tribune Book Review*, November 6, 1960, p.7.

This careful discussion of Rabbit, and his running away from an American way of life, is compared to Dreiser's Griffiths: "Rabbit's floundering in the deadly flypaper of his life has all the force and brilliance of an hallucination."

B144 Serebuick, Judith. *Library Journal*, LXXXV (November 1, 1960), 4009.

This summary makes a recommendation "with reservations": "characters and situations seem curiously out of joint with the lyrical writing and style."

B145 Sherman, Thomas. "Reading and Writing," St. Louis, Mo. *Post-Dispatch*, November 13, 1960, p.4B.

A discussion of Rabbit as a misanthrope, after careful study of plot, suggests that Updike's "feeling for language leads him into extravagant metaphors that . . . add a poetic lustre to a bitter chronicle."

B146 Sinclair, Andrew. "See How He Runs," *Time and Tide,* XLII (September 21, 1961), 1571.

This excellent analysis of Rabbit, mostly on the allegorical level, sees the novel as an "odyssey of a contemporary American in search . . . awareness of the terror of existing along with the blind beauty of the inability to do anything else."

B147 Southern, Terry. "New Trends and Old Hats," *Nation,* CXCI (November 19, 1960), 380.

These are superficial comments with little reference to the novel, suggesting that it relates "the emptiness of self and modern life."

B148 Steiner, George. "In a Rut," *Reporter,* XXIII (December 8, 1960), 81.

There is mention here of Joyce and Nabokov, in relation to Updike's purpose: "He sees in sexual life the only compensation, the only open terrain, left to human beings cornered in the soul-detergent inferno of American middle-class existence."

B149 *Tamarack Review,* (Winter, 1961), 86.

Rather critical of the novel as "flat dramatically," Updike is seen treating sex with frankness and detachment; "a picture of shabby America."

B150 Thompson, John. *Partisan Review,* XXVII (January-February, 1961), 117-124.

This discussion of the novel as picturing the horror of life is critical of Updike for taking too long to make a point: "not a description or a moral lesson, but literally a damnation, and what is damned is all the poor effort of humanity."

B151 Traynor, John. *Extension,* LV (March, 1961), 8.

This brief summary treats the novel as a "shocker" in social comment: ". . . one certainly can't admit that the gloomy sordidness Updike's presented so deftly is the necessary symptom of civilization."

The Magic Flute

B152 Graves, E. M. *Commonweal*, LXXVII (November 16, 1962), 214.
> This is hardly a significant note of description.

B153 Lask, Thomas. *New York Times Book Review*, November 11, 1962, Pt.2, p.62.
> This brief description claims that Updike "has made a pleasant tale out of the libretto."

B154 *Library Journal*, LXXXVII (October 15, 1962), 3896.
> Here is another insignificant note of description.

B155 *Saturday Review*, XLV (December 15, 1962), 28.

Pigeon Feathers

B156 *Best Sellers*, XXII (April 1, 1962), 19.
> This lengthy description, with rather good references to certain stories, suggests that Updike "sees himself with clarity and honesty, and presents his other characters with compassion and kindness. . . ."

B157 "Bigger and Better," *Times Literary Supplement*, February 1, 1963, p.73.
> The praise for these stories indicates that "cleverness is John Updike's bedeviling quality."

B158 *Booklist*, LVIII (April 1, 1962), 522.
> This very brief description offers the claim that Updike's "sensate but still serious approach to human experience is again manifest."

B159 Bradbury, Malcolm. *Punch*, CCLXIV (February 13, 1963), 247.
> This description and comparison to Sherwood Anderson suggests that Updike is "more urbane." "Most of these tales are about the threat to such security that comes from chaos, uncertainty and mystery."

B160 Casey, Genevieve. *Critic*, XX (May, 1962), 76.

A careful description of the collection, with the claim that "stories leave the reader with long thoughts and reveal the dimensions of the person, John Updike, as civilized and sensitive."

B161* Chase, Mary Ellen. "But Can He Communicate?" *New York Herald Tribune Book Review*, March 18, 1962, p.4.

B162 Chester, Alfred. "Twitches and Embarrassments," *Commentary*, XXXIV (July, 1962), 77.

> This is a lengthy and rather sharp dissent on Updike's attitude towards man: "deeply immersed in the image of man as trivia."

B163 Cook, B. A. "A Lesser Form," *Commonweal*, LXXVI (May 11, 1962), 184.

> Although this is not a very thorough study there are notes on patterns in Updike, with autobiographical aspects cited: stories as "limited in their scope and intensity."

B164 Crane, Milton. "Varied, Accomplished Stories With Unifying Themes," Chicago *Sunday Tribune*, April 1, 1962, Pt. IV, p.4.

> Crane briefly reviews past work, and describes this collection: "If the reader finds in such an explanation a moral judgement on a society whose vices are no more deeply felt than its virtues, one suspects that the author will not disagree."

B165 Daniel, John. "Bombardment of Events," *Spectator*, No. 7024 (February 8, 1963), 172.

> This brief analysis has only one specific reference to stories: "Updike's themes are of loss and the fear of death, and of the intelligent young trapped in a ritual which they stare through. . . ."

B166 Didion, Joan. "Books in Brief," *National Review*, XII (June 19, 1962), 452.

> This is merely a brief description of contents: "Updike has an almost shockingly accurate sense of the undertones of common situations."

B167 Diebold, Michael. "Updike Takes Control," Pittsburgh *Press*, May 15, 1962, p.22.

A relation of these stories to past work, with no direct reference, suggests an "over-all communication of the stories as tenderness without sentimentality, poetry without pretension."

B168 Edelstein, J. M. "The Security of Memory," *New Republic*, CXLVI (May 14, 1962), 30.

A discussion, with lengthy quotes, of several stories with the conclusion that stories "dazzle but in their irony, their detachment . . . they display a cleverness and an obvious mannerism that becomes tiresome."

B169* Emerson, Donald. "Three Perceptions," *Progressive*, XXVI (August, 1962), 35.

B170 Hicks, Granville. "Mysteries of the Commonplace," *Saturday Review*, XLV (March 17, 1962), 21-22.

Updike is discussed here as "eagerly in the ardent pursuit of the past." Also a discussion of several stories, with the conclusion that they're not taken seriously "because he so often chooses working with materials that seem slight and commonplace."

B171 Hogan, William. "The Incandescent Updike at Work," San Francisco *Chronicle*, March 22, 1962, p.39.

Here is a reversal of frequent criticism that Updike has nothing to say: "He says plenty by looking for life's meaning in the brief moment, the incidental action, the commonplace."

B172 Hutchens, John. "Pigeon Feathers," New York *Herald Tribune*, March 23, 1962, p.19.

This is a review of Updike's career to date and a description of these stories: "call it the melancholy of a man moving away from his youth."

B173 Hyman, Stanley Edgar. "The Artist as a Young Man," *New Leader*, XLV (March 19, 1962), 22.

Perhaps the best discussion of this collection, with comments on Updike's style and a comparison to Joyce. "Updike's imagery and language are baroque and eloquent." His weakness is seen as his "inability to keep himself out of whatever he writes."

B174 Kansas City *Star*, December 2, 1962, p.G1.

> A brief suggestion that the stories are about "sensitive, middle-class American lives."

B175* *Kirkus*, XXX (January 15, 1962), 71.

B176* Kohler, Dayton. "John Updike Continues to Observe Vagaries of Humanity," Richmond, Va. *News Leader*, March 21, 1962.

B177 Lewis, Arthur. *Books Abroad*, XXXVI (Autumn, 1962), 435.

> This brief description of themes suggests that Updike's success is in his insight: "sometimes sweet, sometimes sad, but always poignant."

B178 "Listen Carefully," *Newsweek*, LIX (March 19, 1962), 120.

> Here is mention of several stories, though none in detail, their relation to the everyday. "Writing like elusive music which exacts the most intent listening."

B179 Maddocks, Melvin. "Updike's Stories," *Christian Science Monitor*, LIV (March 22, 1962), 11.

> A description, and the suggestion of a flaw in Updike's missing a "sense of risk." "These are the almost dangerously virtuosic stories of a brief past."

B180 Mizener, Arthur. "Behind the Dazzle is a Knowing Eye," *New York Times Book Review*, March 18, 1962, pp.1,29.

> An excellent discussion of work, past as well as this, with verbal talent stressed, and a comparison to Joyce. "Updike is the most talented writer of his age in America, and perhaps the most serious."

B181 Morse, J. Mitchell. "Fiction Chronicle," *Hudson Review*, XV (Summer, 1962), 291-302.

> This brief review says little more than that "Updike shows us things and relationships we have gone through life missing."

B182 Novak, Michael. *Commonweal*, LXXVII (February 22, 1963), 577.

A brief comment on themes of middle-class America in Updike's work, this includes an interesting comparison to G. M. Hopkins: that Updike is "recovering Anglo-Saxon sprung rhythm for our prose language."

B183 Parker, Dorothy. *Esquire*, LVII (June, 1962), 66-67.

This very brief description suggests that "Updike reveals too much response to Nature."

B184 Poore, Charles. New York *Times*, March 24, 1962, p. 23.

Here is a description of stories, though with no direct reference, and the suggestion that Updike "examines lives on his sedulously provincial landscape." Also, high praise for craftsmanship.

B185* Pree, Barry. *London Magazine*, III (April, 1963), 87-88.

B186 "Put and Take," *Time*, LXXIX (March 16, 1962), 86.

A rather critical review of Updike because he "does not really seem interested in exploring time and soul." Characterization is discussed briefly; Updike's protagonist seen as the same thin, brooding young man."

B187 Reif, Jane. "Pared Prose in Collection," *Virginian Pilot*, April 29, 1962, p.F6.

These stories are criticized for placing too intellectual a form on the human mold." Also critical of Updike for leaving readers with exquisitely polished skeleton."

B188 Ricks, Christopher. "Tennysonian," *New Statesman*, LXV (February 8, 1963), 208.

An unusually kind review from this source makes an interesting comparison to Victorian literature. The collection is seen as "wry, observant, and stylistically magnetic."

B189 Rowland, S. J. "Limits of Littleness," *Christian Century*, LXXIX (July 4, 1962), 840.

A rather sharp criticism of limitations and of Updike in general, with a comparison to Salinger and Reynolds Price. "The problem is squarely one of Updike's vision . . . we are compelled to recognize his belittling of life."

B190 Serebuick, Judith. *Library Journal*, LXXXVIII (February 15, 1962), 786.

> Updike is briefly discussed here, with few autobiographical aspects cited.

B191* Springfield *Republican*, April 8, 1962, p.4B.

B192 Terral, Rufus. "Brilliant Disturber of Memories," St. Louis, Mo. *Post-Dispatch*, April 1, 1962, p.4C.

> This description of theme and contents offers praise of Updike's talent for taking a trifling incident, telling about it in "densely packed and lacquered poetic prose."

B193 *Virginia Quarterly Review*, LXXXVI (Summer, 1962), lxxvi.

> A suggestion of recurring themes—all aspects of American life—with certain stories cited. Updike is seen here as combining wit and insight, freshness and imagery."

B194 Wathen, Richard. Washington *Post*, March 25, 1962, p.E7.

> A rather brief, insignificant description of themes; there is no direct reference to stories.

B195 *Wisconsin Library Bulletin*, LVIII (July, 1962), 240.

> This is a quick note of enthusiasm for Updike, who is said now to show "a refinement of style."

The Centaur

B196 Adams, Phoebe. *Atlantic*, CCXI (February, 1963), 134.

> A sketchy coverage with a rather sharp criticism of Updike's use of "Victorian Homeric translator's prose."

B197 Adler, Renata. "Arcadia, Pa.," *New Yorker*, XXXIX (April 13, 1963), 182-188.

> This very fine, lucid, and perceptive discussion of the novel offers rare praise for successful use of myth. There is careful interpretation of myth and a summary of plot, with a particular note of praise for "care with which Updike modulates from the key of myth to the key of fact"; also, that his "ob-

servations are acute almost to the point of aphorism." This is one of the best on this work.

B198 Bell, Vivian. "A Study in Frustration," *Shenandoah*, XIV (Summer, 1963), 69-72.

A rather fresh approach, this study of the technical aspects includes the label of post-Joycean in the use of epiphany: "structurally unified and yet thematically incoherent."

B199 *Bookmark*, (December 1, 1963).

This is a very brief note of description.

B200* Black, H. Gilbert. Springfield *Republican*, February 17, 1963.

B201* Bradbury, Malcolm. *Punch*, CCXLV (October 9, 1963), 542.

B202* Brooke, Jordyn. *The Listener*, (October 10, 1963), 577.

B203* Buitenhuis, Peter. *New York Times Book Review*, April 7, 1963, p.4.

B204 Cargas, Harry. *Sign*, XLII (May, 1963), 58.

The reviewer is critical of Updike's lack of plot, for his failing to create a Willy Loman-type character; still "Updike is the most versatile writer in the English language."

B205 Cook, Eleanor. "Turning New Leaves," *Canadian Forum*, XLIII (August, 1963), 113.

The criticism here is focusing upon the use of myth, with a comparison to Iris Murdoch. "Updike is a fundamentalist about his mythology . . . the myth's significance is not really explored, nor is it very relevant to the present."

B206 Crane, Milton. "Classic Myth Refurbished," Chicago *Sunday Tribune*, February 3, 1963, Pt. IV, p.4.

A brief description with the claim of a flaw in implausibility —but, "Updike knows well how to combine spareness and poetry in his prose."

B207 Culligan, Glendy. "Gods Thrive in Pa.," Washington *Post*, February 3, 1963, p.G7.

This detailed summary suggests success despite failure in the use of myth: "Caldwell is a triumph of love and art, perfectly conjoined."

B208 Curley, Thomas. "Between Heaven and Earth," *Commonweal*, LXXVIII (March 29, 1963), 26.

An excellent examination of reasons behind Updike's use of myth AND reality, with much summary and thesis support: "Updike's use of myth is either a frivolity of his fancy or an attempt to will relevance rather than imagine it." A valuable review.

B209 Davenport, Guy. "Novels With Masks," *National Review*, XIV (April 9, 1963), 287-288.

A good capsule criticism and unusual praise for the use of myth, with a comparison to Joyce and Welty. Updike is seen as concerned "to rhyme the adolescent experience of an American high school with the beginning of western education in a Greek gym."

B210 Diebold, Michael. "Updike Novel Ambitious," Pittsburgh *Press*, February 3, 1963, p.8.

The work is described here as a novel but, beyond that, as "a deep and detailed examination of human relationships and values."

B211 Flanagan, Francis. *Ave Maria*, XCVII (March 16, 1963), 25.

This brief summary includes a description of style as "a camara-like recording of details."

B212 Fuller, Edmund. "Reading for Pleasure," *Wall Street Journal*, February 4, 1963, p.14.

Largely a criticism of poor taste, this is a description of theme and myth with contrasting views cited. "The mythic, surrealistic elements create a spell and a hint at the mystery beneath the commonplace."

B213 Gardiner, Harold. *America*, CVIII (March 9, 1963), 340-341.

This summary, with praise for originality, claims that Updike tries to "show how close myth comes to the humdrum world of reality."

B214 Gilman, Richard. "Youth of an Author," *New Republic*, CXLVIII (April 13, 1963), 25.

> A quite critical but quite fine discussion of Updike and of this work as "a complementary vision after . . . the flight from the ogre." Also, a comparison to Salinger: both "resemble those institutionalized national comedians whose references are to their own quirks."

B215 Grauel, G. E. *Best Sellers*, XXII (February 15, 1963), 423.

> This is merely a description, with little comment: "with bold novelty of technique, Updike imposes thin myth on a modern setting."

B216 Guyol, Hazel Sample. "The Lord Loves a Cheerful Corpse," *English Journal*, LV (October, 1966), 863-866.

> A rather thorough study of Geo. Caldwell's personality as central to the novel, this review concentrates on him as a "refreshing and genuine comic creation" who, seeing good in the worst of men, has "no taint of goodness about him." This is quite helpful.

B217 Hicks, Granville. "Pennsylvania Pantheon," *Saturday Review*, LXVI (February 2, 1963), 27-28.

> Critical for failure in use of myth, Hicks includes a summary and sketchy autobiographical aspects. "What Updike seems to be saying is that gods and men are pretty much of a kind."

B218 Hill, W. B. *America*, CVIII (May 11, 1963), 678.

> Here is a very brief description with a note of criticism of the novel's pretentiousness, of poor taste in sex.

B219 Hogan, William. "Greek Myths in a High School Setting," San Francisco *Chronicle*, February 4, 1963, p.31.

> A superficial condemnation of the novel as "an unlikely story."

B220 Hyman, Stanley Edgar. *New Leader*, XLVI (February 4, 1963), 20.

> A rather original analysis of the novel as compared to Joyce's *Ulysses*, this cites autobiographical elements: "Updike's com-

pulsive preoccupation with his adolescence is like a questing back to innocence."

B221 *Jubilee,* XI (December, 1963), 52.

Although critical of novel for its failure to be an epic, this sees Updike as a craftsman: "the sheer weight of exquisite detail in his stories seems to dwarf the characters."

B222 Kansas City *Star,* February 3, 1963, p.3E.

In this very brief note Caldwell is called a "Christ-like father."

B223 Kirsch, Robert. "National Awards Criticized," Los Angeles *Times,* March 11, 1964, p.4.

Although written as a comment on the National Book Awards, this should be noted as a review. There is no reference to theme or plot here, but sharp criticism of Updike as a "fine craftsman with a narrow and slender vision."

B224* Kluger, Richard. *New York Herald Tribune Book Review,* April 7, 1963, p.8.

B225 Kuehn, Robert. *Wisconsin Studies in Contemporary Literature,* V (Winter-Spring, 1964), 77-78.

A brief discussion of Updike as a "genre artist," and highly critical of myth employed: "the method of alternating one mode of experience with another seems oddly naive."

B226 Lewis, Arthur. *Books Abroad,* XXXVII (Summer, 1963), 340.

There is not much reference to the novel but a suggestion of "failure either to treat the story objectively or to push the myth further."

B227 Malin, Irving. "Occasions for Loving," *Kenyon Review,* XXV (Spring, 1963), 348-352.

A study of images in the work—"he captures sensations, not complex relationships"—Updike is seen here describing "occasions for loving."

B228 Miller, Jonathan. "Off-Centaur," *New York Review of Books,* I (No. 1, 1963), 28.

This is a good, comprehensive discussion, with comparison to

Bellow, Joyce, and Hemingway. "If the allegorical theme is announced too clearly the irony becomes monotonous and the art gives way to pedantry."

B229 Minetree, Harry. "From Olinger, Pa. to Mt. Olympus," St. Louis, Mo. *Post-Dispatch*, March 24, 1963, p.4C.
This brief summary, with a comparison to Salinger, questions the use of myth; suggests novel as commendable "tour de force."

B230* Murrey, J. G. *Critic*, XXI (March, 1963), 72.

B231 "A Mystical Animal," *Times Literary Supplement*, September 27, 1963, p.728.
This is perhaps the most praiseworthy review of the novel, as "outstandingly good." Success is said to be in use of myth, in the character of Caldwell, and in the extension of the myth to Peter.

B232 Nordell, Roderick. "An Updike Mythology," *Christian Science Monitor*, LV (February 7, 1963), 7.
Critical of mythmaking, Nordell praises Updike's evoking of "family relationships with a poet's delicacy and concreteness.

B233 Pickrel, Paul. *Harper's*, CCXXVI (April, 1963), 92.
Although critical of the use of myth, the claim is for Updike as "best novelist of his generation." Previous novels are cited briefly.

B234 Podhoretz, Norman. "A Dissent on Updike," *Show*, III (April, 1963), 49-52. (See B7)
This brief study of Caldwell discusses the entire novel as too unclear: "a self-conscious effort at brilliance."

B235 Prescott, Orville. New York *Times*, February 4, 1963, p.7.
Although not much summary, there is a discussion of myth and a comparison to Joyce. "Updike is still feeling his way, still groping for his own natural means of expression." The novel is seen as "image of pretentious experimentation."

B236 Price, Martin. "Seven Recent Novels," *Yale Review*, LII (Summer, 1963), 601-610.

Critical of Updike for attempting Joyce and resulting in Wilder, Price includes a summary of plot and theme: "with fine precision Updike shows pains turning into sweetness."

B237 "Prometheus Unsound," *Time*, LXXXI (February 8, 1963), 83.

A quick and rather superficial summary of plot, and criticism of the use of myth: "Updike's enormous unbalanced metaphor eventually topples off the edge of audacity into preciousness."

B238 Roberts, Preston. *Christian Century*, LXXX (April 10, 1963), 463.

This is a study of the novel as, simply, one about death; "humor, realism, poetry and a profoundly tragic sense of life."

B239 Sale, Roger. "Gossips and Storytellers," *Hudson Review*, XVI (Spring, 1963), 141-149.

There is more comment here on Updike's maturity than on the novel: his "talent for always knowing what a character will say or do is the sign of a growing and human imagination."

B240 Serebuick, Judith. *Library Journal*, LXXXVIII (January 15, 1963), 238.

This study of Caldwell and his relation to other fathers in Updike's work includes a quick summation, with autobiographical elements cited.

B241 Steiner, George. *Reporter*, XXVIII (March 14, 1963), 52.

A study of the novel as a deviation from previous work, comparison is made here to Joyce and Nabokov. "The book belongs to a genre that crops up in the Renaissance but whose place in English fiction has always been marginal and somewhat embarrassed: an allegorical novel."

B242* Stern, Richard. *Spectator*, No. 7056 (September 27, 1963), 389.

B243 Taubman, Robert. "God is Delicate," *New Statesman*, LXVI (September 27, 1963), 406.

A scholarly discussion of the novel on a philosophical level, rather than plot outline. "One more attempt to purge American life of its grossness." Also, comparison to Joyce, Miller.

B244 "Updikemanship," *Newsweek*, LXI (February 11, 1963), 91.

With more summation than analysis, this is a study of Caldwell as a "dreary jerk," but Updike's triumph is seen in his presenting "the courage and buoyant goodness of his (Caldwell's) character."

B245 *Virginia Quarterly Review*, XXXIX (Spring, 1963), vlviii.

A brief but lucid comment on Updike's performance: "deeply moving, richly allegorical and profoundly tragic reinterpretation of the myth of Chiron in modern times."

Telephone Poles

B246 "American Poetry's Casual Look," London *Times*, January 7, 1965, p.13C.

An extremely brief note of description of the collection as "almost Victorian word-play."

B247* Black, Gilbert. Springfield *Republican*, November 3, 1963.

B248 Burns, R. K. *Library Journal*, LXXXVIII (October 1, 1963), 3628.

This is merely a brief suggestion that "Updike continues to have fun with the absurdities that occur in daily existence."

B249 Callahan, Patrick. "The Poetry of Imperfection," *Prairie Schooner*, XXXIX (Winter, 1965-1966), 364-365.

The collection is discussed as "almost holy," and Updike as both playful and serious; he neither "avant-gardes his readers to death nor chokes them in metaphysics."

B250 Fendel, John. "7 Poets: The Creation of Images to Delight," *Commonweal*, LXXX (May 8, 1964), 212.

A very short description, with a reference to several poems;

"Updike is agile in using words and has a lot of fun being funny."

B251 Fuller, Edmund. "The Versatile Updike," *Wall Street Journal*, October 31, 1963, p.16.

This is perhaps the most thorough review of this work, and prophetic of Updike's future as a serious poet. Reference is made to and excerpts taken from several poems. "7 Stanzas at Easter" discussed as a "profound and masterfully-wrought religious poem."

B252 Keister, Donald. "Updike's *Telephone Poles* Soars to a Beautiful Climax," Cleveland *Plain Dealer*, September 22, 1963, p.7H.

There is not much reference to poetry, but a conclusion reached is that "the mood throughout is one of acceptance of man, nature, and all their works."

B253 Kennedy, X. J. "A Light Look at Today," *New York Times Book Review*, September 22, 1963, p.10.

A discussion of the poetry, with excerpts, as describing "the small absurdities we live with daily in this world of technology."

B254 Lask, Thomas. New York *Times*, September 21, 1963, p.19.

This description of themes makes interesting comparison to Dame Edith Sitwell: "playfulness of ideas is matched by the sportiveness of the lines."

B255 "Light Fantastic," *Time*, LXXXII (November 1, 1963), 112.

This brief review, with lengthy excerpts, makes comparison to Britain's John Betjeman. Updike as "able to slip unobtrusively out of light verse into something more barbed."

B256 Moody, Minnie. "Promise Unfulfilled in New Updike Poems," Columbus *Dispatch*, December 8, 1963, p.D23.
This is a rather insignificant comment on style.

B257 Ricks, Christopher. "Spotting Syllabics," *New Statesman*, LXVII (May 1, 1964), 685.

A brief comment sees Updike's poems as condoning "too much in their wish to make people frown."

B258 "Rustic and Urban," *Times Literary Supplement,* August 20, 1964, p.748.

An interesting contrast with James Dickey, with the latter preferred for seriousness. Updike seen here as "urbane, witty, well-read," but a poet of trivia.

B259 Schott, Webster. "Any Idea May be Shaped Into Poetry," Kansas City *Star*, December 2, 1963, p.28.

These are very slight comments on the verse as "admirably suited to the smallness of his topics."

B260* Silver, Mildred. St. Louis *Globe*, October 19, 1963.

B261 Simpson, Louis. "Don't Take a Poem by the Horn," *Book Week*, October 27, 1963, pp.6,25.

An insignificant and brief description, this rather sharp criticism sees poetry as a "waste of time."

B262 Spector, Robert. *Saturday Review*, XLVII (February 1, 1964), 38.

There is brief comparison to other poets, and "sophomoric sophistication in overly clever rhymes" is noted here.

B263 Stitt, Peter. "Let Bobo be Bubo," *Minnesota Review*, IV (Winter, 1964), 268-271.

A sharp criticism, with several excerpts to support the argument that Updike's "sense of poetic technique is at best superficial," sees poetry as flat, lacking wit.

B264 Tazewell, William. "Author Updike: A Poet at Play," *Virginian Pilot*, October 6, 1963, p.B6.

High praise is given for "McGinley-type" poetry, with reference to poems and excerpts. "Updike finds subjects of verse in the appurtenances of suburbia and the circumstances of life's trivia."

The Ring

B265 *Christian Science Monitor*, LVI (November 5, 1964), 8B.

This is perhaps the best description and comment on this work. One weakness found is that "sentences are likely to whizz velvetly by all but the most Jacobin moppets."

B266 Dagliesh, Alice. *Saturday Review*, XLVII (November 7, 1964), 52.

This is merely a note of description.

B267 Lask, Thomas. *New York Times Book Review*, November 1, 1964, p.63.

Perhaps the longest description available, this notes that Updike's version "is not a synopsis of Wagner's libretto."

B268 Morse, J. C. *Horn Book*, XLI (February, 1965), 71.

Another mere description of contents.

B269 Sheehan, Ethna. *America*, CXI (November 21, 1964), 671.

Here is a description of the "picture book" indicating its value as a child's book.

B270 Wagner, M. K. *Library Journal*, LXXXIX (December 15, 1964), 5012.

These brief notes of praise claim that Updike "gives enough detail from earlier and later events to cover the entire range of Wagner's epic."

Olinger Stories

Although the following review is the only one located for this volume, it is considered valuable enough to warrant this separate section in the list.

B271 Overall, Nadine. "John Updike: *Olinger Stories*, A Selection," *Studies in Short Fiction*, IV (Winter, 1967), 195-197.

Although little analysis of the stories, there is interesting reference to autobiographical aspects, to other criticism, and to quotes by Updike. One comment on style: "keen perceptiveness plus verbal adroitness, both personified, equal John Updike."

B272 Dagliesh, Alice. *Saturday Review*, XLIX (January 22, 1966), 45.

> This is a brief description with a note on "direct, pleasant, though in no way unusual verses."

B273 Dickey, James. *New York Times Book Review*, November 7, 1965, p.6.

> These are the lengthiest comments on this work; Updike as having failed in "too much sense of clever oversimplification about his verse," as straining for child's approval.

B274 Eaton, Anne. *Commonweal*, LXXXIII (November 5, 1965), 157.

> Merely another note of description, this is insignificant.

B275 Lurie, Alison. *New York Review of Books*, V (December 9, 1965), 39.

> The suggestion here is that verse is "really addressed to nostalgic grownups, not children."

B276 Maxwell, Emily. *New Yorker*, XLI (December 4, 1965), 232.

> A brief description of the poems as corresponding to the seasons, "like something suddenly remembered."

B277 Pryce-Jones, Alan. "More Than Just Child's Play," *Book Week*, October 31, 1965, p.7.

> These are very brief, superficial comments on poems as "crystal simplicity."

B278 "The Updike Year," *Christian Science Monitor*, LVII (November 4, 1965), B2.

> Here is a very good review suggesting, with summary of contents, that Updike "trades unashamedly, though with remarkable freshness, on American staples."

Verse

B279 Allen, Morse. "Worth the Money," Hartford *Courant*, May 2, 1965, Magazine Sec., p.13.

A brief and rather superficial coverage, dividing verse into "comic" and "tragic" departments.

B280 "Brattish, Maybe, But Not At All Banal," Springfield, Ohio *Sun*, April 17, 1965.

A very interesting treatment of collection in relation to the history of "light verse," the latter as quite serious: "society verse or familiar verse, it is highly sophisticated . . . marked by delicacy of touch and subtle wit." Updike as a "master" at verse, as well as a "major novelist."

B281 Cromie, Robert. "John Updike Poetry Put Into New Volume," Chicago *Tribune*, February 16, 1965, Sec. 2, p.2.

A rather comprehensive survey of the collection, this praises Updike for communicating "deftly, wittily, whimsically, superbly."

B282 Fremont-Smith, Eliot. "End Papers," New York *Times*, February 18, 1965, p.31.

Short praise is offered here for range of poems, from "playfully satirical light verse to elegant and powerful evocations of innocence and loss."

B283 Taylor, Michael. "Collected Poems Now in Paperback," Nashville, Tenn. *Banner*, April 2, 1965, p.28.

A comparison to Auden includes the suggestion of "universal importance, a flash of insight that somehow makes the incident that inspired the poem less vital than the poetic conclusion."

B284 "Updike's Poems Are Real," Boston *Traveler*, February 12, 1965.

Although this is quite superficial, there is the suggestion that poems are "impeccable, funny, droll, wistful, heart-smashing, true."

B285 "Updike Best at Verse," Denver, Colo. *Rocky Mountain News*, February 14, 1965, p.26A.

This is as much criticism of Updike as a novelist—of "restricted vision." Light poems are preferred; others said to "waver perilously between sentimentality and triteness."

B286 Binns, F. W. *Library Journal*, XC (May 15, 1965), 2264.

> This is merely a description, a run-down on the table of contents.

B287 Fremont-Smith, Eliot. "An Adventurer on Behalf of Us All," New York *Times*, June 23, 1965, p.39.

> Although there is little said of this work, this is an excellent discussion of reasons behind Updike's failure to become popular with critics: "he is not exotic . . . he is unfashionable and inconvenient . . . to trend hunters." This is certainly perceptive and worth while.

B288 "The Gymnist," *Newsweek*, LXV (May 17, 1965), 108.

> Not a detailed discussion but an interesting comment on the influence of Nabokov and the nostalgia of Agee, this sees Updike as doing "fancy figure skating on his frozen flux."

B289 Hamlin, William. "A Harvest of Updike," St. Louis, Mo. *Post-Dispatch*, September 5, 1965, p.4B.

> Another rather superficial, though lengthy, description of contents.

B290 Hicks, Granville. "They Also Serve Who Write Well," *Saturday Review*, XLVIII (May 15, 1965), 25.

> Hicks discusses past work as well as this, with autobiographical aspects noted as well as background reviewed. "Updike's versatility is as obvious as his mastery of the language."

B291 Kay, J. H. "Casuals by Updike," *Christian Science Monitor*, LVII (June 26, 1965), 9.

> A rather critical criticism of this assortment as "motley . . . one looks in vain to isolate the real Updike."

B292 Kenny, Herbert. "Updike's Essays Show Variety and Style," Boston *Globe*, May 24, 1965, p.14.

> This careful description of contents concludes that this form is superior to fiction: "There is about his novels a touch of the bizarre which indicates a basic covert dissatisfaction with the form." This is one of the best reviews of this work.

B293 Morgan, Thomas. "A Casual Collection," *New York Times Book Review*, June 13, 1965, p.10.

> This description of contents concludes that in the reviews included "one begins to get an insight into what Updike thinks he has been saying all this time . . . about his own spiritual crisis."

B294 Newman, Charles. "Journalistic Exercises," Chicago *Tribune*, May 23, 1965, Sec. IX, p.12.

> This is a brief description of contents, but mostly a defense of attacks on *New Yorker* style.

B295 "On Demand," *Time*, LXXXV (May 21, 1965), 113.

> A brief, rather critical review of "the collage assembled beneath this arrogantly stark title."

Of The Farm

B296 Aldridge, John. "Cultivating Corn Out of Season," *Book Week*, November 21, 1965, p.5.

> A rather ambiguous discussion of Updike as a gifted writer having no characteristics of one; also, notes on three other novels and the conclusion that "Updike has nothing to say."

B297 Berolzheimer, H. F. *Library Journal*, XC (December 1, 1965), 5303.

> This is a brief recommendation, with the suggestion of the novel as a sequel to *The Centaur.*

B298 *Best Sellers*, XXV (February 1, 1966), 420.

> A rather superficial description of the contents and the action as autobiographical: "There is no real solution of the many problems exposed."

B299 Buitenhuis, Peter. "The Mowing of a Meadow," *New York Times Book Review*, November 14, 1965, p.4.

> This summary of plot praises the use of symbolism: "He has seen his subject and shaped his form with a clarity that leaves his reader with a sense of inevitable rightness."

B300 Casey, Florence. "Updike's Trap of Freedom," *Christian Science Monitor*, LVII (November 18, 1965), 15.

In this rather original discussion, including a plot summary, the Mother-Son relationship is studied, and Updike's question is seen as: "how to take any initiative without impinging upon another's liberty."

B301 Culligan, Glendy. "Updike is Back on the Farm With a Luminous Novel," Washington *Post*, November 23, 1965, p.A22.

A very interesting relation of this work to Updike's background results in rare praise for the novel: "Updike narrows the wide river of human experience to a trickle of event, each incident condensing a more universal past."

B302* Epstein, Joseph. *New Republic*, CLIII (December 11, 1965), 23.

B303 "Four-Ring Circus," *Newsweek*, LXVI (November 15, 1965), 129A.

This "flowery" review contains much summary: "He is a minor master at creating detailed human portraits of serene desperation or muted catastrophe."

B304 French, Warren. "Updike Turns Back from Ambitious Mythology," Kansas City *Star*, November 14, 1965, p. 10F.

The novel is briefly discussed as "an idyll of the dying countryside," but the rather technical criticism dwells upon insignificant points.

B305 Hicks, Granville. "Mothers, Sons and Lovers," *Saturday Review*, XLVIII (November 13, 1965), 41.

A rather paradoxical review in which the novel is discussed as lacking a "mighty theme," yet credit is given for its being "subtle and profound." A fine summation, with conclusion that the subject might seem "rather slight even to Henry James."

B306 Klein, Marcus. "A Mouse in the Barn," *Reporter*, XXXIII (December 16, 1965), 54.

This discussion of symbolism in the novel sees Updike as less deft than in previous works. "The materials upon which Updike practices are inherently pathetic."

B307* Kohler, Dayton. Richmond, Va. *News Leader*, December 1, 1965.

B308 Kort, Wesley. *Christian Century*, LXXXIII (January 19, 1966), 82.
> An interesting analysis of the novel as "a confession of debt": "Updike's own debt to a concrete reality"; Joey Robinson seen as "maintaining an alternative to death."

B309 L'Heureux, John. *Critic*, XXIV (January, 1966), 64.
> This indictment of Updike as over-rated gives a brief description of the novel and the judgement that it "is his simplest and best."

B310 Lindroth, J. R. *America*, CXIII (November 27, 1965), 692.
> The novel is discussed here as symbolic, with a comparison to Henry James. Updike is seen as now revealing "wit, complexity of characterization, nuance of style."

B311 Moore, Harry T. "Static Exercise in Technique," Pittsburgh *Press*, December 5, 1965, p.12.
> This rather bland discussion sees the novel as "more like a report than a novel."

B312 "Narrowing Compass," *Time*, LXXXVI (November 12, 1965), 118.
> Here is a quick summation and criticism of the novel as "too brief, inactive and unambitious."

B313 Poore, Charles. "Joey at 35," New York *Times*, November 20, 1965, p.33.
> This very brief criticism includes an illustration of the novel as "needlessly embellished with touches of hand-painted china style."

B314 Ragan, Lawrence. *Extension*, LX (February, 1966), 47.
> Updike is seen here as reflecting life: "He refuses to simplify; he is unwilling to reduce his characters to stereotypes that will find comfortable grooves in the reader's mind."

B315 Sale, Roger. "High Mass and Low Requiem," *Hudson Review*, XIII (Spring, 1966), 124-134.

There is not a very thorough discussion of this novel, and only small space devoted to Updike in this coverage of several writers. A suggestion made is that Updike "seems badly in need of new subject"; Joey is seen as Caldwell, the younger, 20 years later.

B316 Seward, William. "Reunion at Farm Attracts Ghosts, Too," *Virginian Pilot*, November 21, 1965, p.B4.

This rather negative review, with summation and excerpts, suggests the novel as "a sound stylistic performance in spite of the author's use of idiosyncratic syntax."

B317* Springfield *Republican*, January 30, 1966.

B318 Sullivan, Richard. "A Quartet of Tangled Actors," Chicago *Tribune*, November 28, 1965, Sec. IX, p.6.

This is a brief and rather paradoxical review of the novel as "brilliantly weak, it is so manifestly a complex piece of remarkable writing which fails."

B319 Thompson, John. "Matthiessen and Updike," *New York Review of Books*, V (December 23, 1965), 23.

There is more on Matthiessen, but criticism of Updike is based upon other critics' concession at not understanding him. Any plot seen as being "rigged beneath the elegantly presented surface of three uneventful, homely days."

B320* *U. S. Catholic*, XXXI (February, 1966), 65.

B321 Weeks, Edward. "The Duel on the Farm," *Atlantic*, CCXVI (December, 1965), 138.

This short account is mostly summation of plot, with only a hint of analysis of Updike as "a stylist with a sure touch."

The Music School

B322 Adams, Robert. "Without Risk," *New York Times Book Review*, September 18, 1966, pp.4-5.

A description of themes, those familiar to Updike, these are merely comments on "delicate perception and precise expression."

B323 Alverez, Paul. "Updike Collection Swings," Pittsburgh *Press*, September 18, 1966, Sec.8, p.6.

> With several references to the stories, a comparison is made to Fitzgerald in the way of "recording how people lived, how they thought and how they reacted in suburban society."

B324 Appel, David. "Updike Vignettes, Perelman Parodies," Philadelphia *Inquirer*, September 18, 1966, Sec.7, p.7.

> Although most attention is paid Perelman—admittedly the reviewer's favorite—there are descriptive notes on Updike's stories and suggestion of his "ability to pinpoint human character, despite all its elusiveness."

B325 *Booklist*, LX (October 15, 1966), 236.

> This is a brief note on the stories as "notable in their realization of natural scenes and the emotion and thought of individuals."

B326 Casey, Florence. "Tiny Happenings of Near-Events," *Christian Science Monitor*, LVIII (September 22, 1966), 11.

> The stories are seen here as episodic, as out of touch with the times: "like those of Salinger and Roth, Updike's world focuses exclusively on the problems of the American middle class."

B327 Cook, Roderick. *Harper's*, CCXXXIII (September, 1966), 113.

> These brief comments see stories as typically *New Yorker* in style: "poetical, comical, tragical, pastoral, metropolitan."

B328 *Critic*, XXV (October, 1966), 116.

> Another very brief note on the stories as surrounded on "all four sides by the *New Yorker*."

B329 Dilts, Susan. "Updike in a Deep Rut," Baltimore *Sunday Sun*, October 2, 1966, p.D9.

> There is praise of style here but criticism of Updike's failure to "say something . . . in none of the stories do any potentially dramatic and tragic themes mean much to us, because the people are so lacking in any kind of distinction."

B330 Hicks, Granville. "Domestic Felicity?" *Saturday Review*, XLIX (September 24, 1966), 31.

> Partly a discussion of Bruce Jay Friedman and partly a comparison or relation of this work to other work by Updike; emphasis here is upon one story: "Christian Roommates."

B331 Hubler, Richard. "Updike Dazzles Until It's Boresome," Los Angeles *Times*, September 25, 1966, p.28.

> This discussion sees Updike as a writer for a selected few. Also, a brief description: "empathy, as delicate and as evanescent as a scent in summer."

B332 Jacobsen, Josephine. *Commonweal*, LXXXV (December 9, 1966), 299-300.

> Another description of themes, with a comparison to Graham Greene. Updike is seen as having "explored more accurately the terrible middle ground—the disastrous area of circumstance, where body and spirit are alike defeated."

B333 "John and Bruce," *Newsweek*, LXVIII (September 26, 1966), 116.

> Contrasted with Bruce Jay Friedman, Updike is pictured "tender, lyrical as Lermontov." Some stories are cited, and conclusion reached is that each writer has a different "reaction to modern society's aches and pains."

B334 Kuicheloe, H. G. "Updike's Skill Shows in Stories," Raleigh *News and Observer*, August 21, 1966, Sec.3, p.3.

> This is simply a description of contents.

B335* Light, Carolyn. *Best Sellers*, XXVI (October 1, 1966), 240.

B336 Macauley, Robie. "Cartoons and Arabesques," *Book Week*, September 25, 1966, p.4.

> This sharp criticism of Updike for "doing fine penmanship around familiar characters," includes another comparison to Friedman.

B337 "Madrigals from a Rare Bird," *Time*, LXXXVIII (September 23, 1966), 105.

> Emphasis here is upon lyricism and upon Updike's maturity:

"no longer transfixed by the pool of childhood memories . . . interested in the faces looking over the shoulder of Narcissus."

B338 McNamara, Eugene. *America*, CXV (October 15, 1966), 462.

These are short comments on the stories and on Updike's "ability to render scenes from our own usual, tawdry and familiar world."

B339 Meinke, Peter. "Yearning for Yesteryear," *Christian Century*, LXXXIII (December 7, 1966), 1512.

Updike and his stories are discussed here as moral and religious: "The emptiness of modern life, echoing through these tales, is connected with loss of faith."

B340 Minerof, Arthur. *Library Journal*, XCI (September 15, 1966), 4137.

This brief discussion of themes places emphasis upon characterization: "interrelationships among many of the characters, and they appear duplicates or complements of each other."

B341 Newman, Charles. "Top Talent Taking it Easy," Chicago *Tribune*, September 11, 1966, Sec. IX, p.8.

This criticism suggests a decline: "adolescent sentimentality and forced intellectual allusions exist side by side."

B342 *Playboy*, XIII (November, 1966).

A brief reference is made to one story and few significant comments on Updike, other than: "he is adept at exposing the nerves and muscles of an emotion."

B343* Robertson, Donald. Cleveland *Plain Dealer*, September 18, 1966.

B344 Samuels, Charles Thomas. *Commonweal*, LXXXV (December 2, 1966), 272.

This is merely a note of recommendation.

B345 Samuels, Charles Thomas. *Nation*, CCIII (October 3, 1966), 328.

Here is a fine discussion of this collection and a defense of Updike's seriousness, of his writing of un-fulfilled love: "His seriousness is chastened by modesty, his nostalgia is both joyful and unillusioned, his precision is both linguistic and dramatic."

B346* *Status*, (November, 1966), 8.

B347 Weeks, Edward. *Atlantic*, CCXVIII (November, 1966), 154-156.

There are few specific references here, but much praise for Updike as "one of the most skillful practitioners of this art."

B348 Wells, Joel. "Updike Runs . . . On and On," *Extension*, LXI (October, 1966), 54-55.

This brief description includes much comment on Updike's style: "at its best, it is a subtle and fine meshed net with which he sometimes seines the most elusive and deepest-swimming truths about humanity."

B349 Zane, Maitland. "An Updike Collection: Emotions Laid Raw," San Francisco *Chronicle*, September 18, 1966, p. 38.

There is high praise here for Updike as "virtuoso," with a description of stories. "Updike is sensitive to nuances of colors, settings, especially man-woman relationships."